WOMAN of CONFIDENCE

Wisdom for Achieving with Integrity

PAM FARREL

InterVarsity Press
Downers Grove, Illinois

InterVarsity Press
P.O. Box 1400, Downers Grove, IL 60515-1426
World Wide Web: www.ivpress.com
E-mail: mail@ivpress.com

InterVarsity Press® is the book-publishing division of InterVarsity Christian Fellowship/USA®, a student movement active on campus at hundreds of universities, colleges and schools of nursing in the United States of America, and a member movement of the International Fellowship of Evangelical Students. For information about local and regional activities, write Public Relations Dept., InterVarsity Christian Fellowship/USA, 6400 Schroeder Rd., P.O. Box 7895, Madison, WI 53707-7895, or visit the IVCF website at <www.ivcf.org>.

All Scripture quotations, unless otherwise indicated, are taken from the Holy Bible, New International Version®. NIV®. *Copyright ©1973, 1978, 1984 by International Bible Society. Used by permission of Zondervan Publishing House. All rights reserved.*

Cover illustration: Claude Monet, Garden at Giverny/Österreichische Galerie Bevedere

ISBN 0-8308-2248-8

Printed in the United States of America ∞

Library of Congress Cataloging-in-Publication Data

Farrel, Pam, 1959-
    Woman of confidence: wisdom for achieving with integrity / Pam Farrel.
       p. cm.
    Includes bibliographical references.
    ISBN 0-8308-2248-8 (pbk. : alk. paper)
       1. Christian women—Religious life. 2. Success—Religious aspects—Christianity. 3.
    Confidence—Religious aspects—Christianity. I. Title.
    BV4527 .F49 2001
    48.8'43—dc12

                                                                                    2001039357

25 24 23 22 21 20 19 18 17 16 15 14 13 12 11 10 9 8 7 6 5 4 3 2 1

22 21 20 19 18 17 16 15 14 13 12 11 10 09 08 07 06 05 04 03 02 01

To my friend and mentor, Vyonda

*I gained confidence
because you lived out God's Word
every day, in every way.*

*You taught us
how to live,
how to love,
and how to die.*

*Blessed is the one who perseveres under trial,
because when she has stood the test, she will receive the crown of
life that God has promised to those who love him. . . .
And when the Chief Shepherd appears, you will receive the crown
of glory that will never fade away. . . .
Be faithful, even to the point of death, and I will give you
the crown of life. (Jas 1:12 paraphrased; 1 Pet 5:4; Rev 2:10)*

$\mathscr{C}$ONTENTS

Preface

Do you ever feel not-so-confident, like your past was nothing special and your future seems unclear?

Woman of Confidence seeks to change your thinking about life by looking at the lives of real women—women who have achieved because they relied upon God and followed his standards rather than their own. Each chapter examines a key word from the motivational movement and defines it in terms of God's eternal and unchanging character.

As you travel through the pages of this book, keep a journal handy. Each chapter ends with "Winning Words"—portions of Scripture strung together and personalized so that you can wrap your heart around the power of God's Word. Record your favorite verses in your journal as personal encouragement from God's heart to your own. You can also use Winning Words to pray for yourself and others when they need confidence. Each chapter will also have a section called "Winning Ways" filled with practical exercises to strengthen you for the journey ahead—a journey of achievement. In your journal, you can write down your thoughts and answers to the questions in these sections.

At the end of the book, I have included a brief discussion of accountability partners, or what I call fine-tuning friends. If you already have an accountability partner, study this book together, discuss it at lunch or over e-mail and ask the hard question, "How are you going to apply what you learned? How are you going to apply it today, this week, this month?" The sooner you implement the principles, the sooner God can weave integrity, confidence and achievement into your life.

As you read *Woman of Confidence,* I hope you take the time to reflect upon your own life and see how God is working through you to achieve his purposes for your future. It is my prayer that this book will point you to the character of God and be the catalyst you need to become a woman of confidence.

I am confident of this, that the one who began a good work among you will bring it to completion by the day of Jesus Christ. (Phil 1:6 NRSV)

1

*C*ONFIDENCE

"You can't, God never said you could.
God can, He always said He would."
JILL BRISCOE

*W*hen we were newlyweds, my husband and I were challenged to leave our thriving youth ministry, our cozy church and our long-time friends and head off to seminary. I didn't want to go. I cried for hours the night we were challenged to uproot and move. The seminary was located in the heart of Los Angeles, and for me, a farm girl, living in the suburbs had been a stretch. I saw Los Angeles as a hostile environment—I wasn't even sure God existed in Los Angeles!

But I knew I couldn't live with the stress I was feeling. I couldn't go around with swollen eyes from crying, a sullen attitude or the feeling of fear and dread that accompanied me like a black cloud. I called an older friend, Barbara, who was the mother of one of my best friends. Barbara had been around the world, accompanying her husband to dangerous and exotic countries, with three tiny children in tow. I thought if anyone knew how to make the pain inside my heart go away, she would. (And I was secretly hoping she'd say, "Oh, sweetie, you're right, I'm sure God's not calling you into a hostile place like Los Angeles.")

I showed up at Barbara's home at three o'clock in the afternoon and didn't leave until nine o'clock that evening. That's a lot of time for Barbara to give—but I needed it. I needed the medicine she gave. But it wasn't a pep talk or a motivational "can do" hype. To my surprise, Barbara didn't take my side. Instead she confirmed my calling. And then she went one step further—she recounted to me the faithfulness of God in her life. She walked me through the character and faithfulness of God, hour after hour, example after example. Over dinner, Barbara recounted to me the faithfulness of God in her life. Over ice cream, Barbara recounted to me the faithfulness of God in her life. And as we returned to her home, Barbara continued to recount to me the faithfulness of God.

That night when my husband came to pick me up, I walked through the doors of Barbara's home with confidence, knowing I could walk through any door God opened. I embraced God's faithfulness and unchanging character, and I felt like a new woman—a woman of confidence.

A New Attitude

Women—people—are desperate for confidence. A quick perusal of the Internet produces hundreds of self-esteem building sites. "All in all, we are not very confident by nature. Ninety percent of our thoughts about ourselves are negative," says Alice Domar, Ph.D., director of the Mind/ Body Center for Women's Health at Harvard Medical School.[1] It has been estimated that almost 90 percent of college students feel inferior in some way.[2] Self-defeating behavior is the single most common reason that people seek psychotherapy, according to Mark Goulston, M.D. Dr. Goulston explains that some of us are raised to be more confident than others: "If when things go wrong for a child their parents respond angrily or fearfully, they're more likely to grow up feeling . . . insecure." Lack of confidence seriously affects a majority of women. According to the *Journal of the American Medical Association*, depression is expected to be the second leading cause of disability worldwide in the next decade.[3]

Our self-confidence is so fragile that according to a Yale University researcher's study, even a bad hair day affects us! On those bad hair days we feel less smart, less capable, more embarrassed and less sociable.[4]

What's the key? What unlocks a person's potential without harming the person's psyche? What is the secret to real success, staying power and fulfillment? How can we achieve, maybe achieve greatly and still maintain our integrity? How can we develop the confidence to walk into our hopes, dreams and aspirations?

There is nothing more vital, more central to your own self-confidence than your confidence in God.

"The truth is self-confident people aren't necessarily brimming with talent, skill, or physical beauty; they just feel they are," continues Dr. Goulston, "They think differently than their less assured peers, especially when faced with loss, defeat, or uncertainty."[5] Confident women think differently. It's my experience, and my observation, that confident women think differently because they think different thoughts—not their own, but God's. The confidence of their life is rooted in the most primary of all relationships—a relationship with God. We can become women of confidence only as we grasp a great view of God.

We can become women of confidence only as we grasp a great view of God.

There is nothing more vital, more central to your own self-confidence than your confidence in God. A.W. Tozer, in *Knowledge of the Holy*, says, "What comes into our minds when we think about God is the most important thing about us."[6] Henry Blackaby and Claude King agree. In their work entitled *Experiencing God* they write, "How I live my life is a testimony of what I believe about God."[7] I like to say "Show me your God, and I will show you your ability to achieve. Small God—small life. Big God—big opportunities and potential await." Too many of us, however, do not see God for who he really is. J. B. Phillips, in *Your God is Too Small*, explains the quandary many of us find ourselves in:

> We are modeling God upon what we know of man. That is why it is con-
> tended here that what at first sight appears to be almost a super adequate
> idea of God is, in reality, inadequate—it is based on too tiny a foundation.
> Man may be made in the image of God; but it is not sufficient to conceive
> God as nothing more than infinitely magnified man.[8]

Seeing God as merely an elevated form of ourselves sets us up for failure. We miss out on all God has for us because we fail to see him as the all-powerful, all-knowing, all-loving God who provides for all our needs. But when we realize that God is more than a man, when we examine his unchanging character, we gain confidence in him and in his love for us. We become confident that he will work in and through us.

The Shortcut Comes Up Short

Ann, a woman in my ministry, came to me one day very upset. It seems one of her employees, Susan, who was also a good friend, was on the verge of a nervous breakdown. Susan, wanting to achieve and get ahead in life, had been overdosing on self-help motivational tapes. Over and over again she was told, "You can do it. You can do it." In reality Susan couldn't do it. "It" was causing her to lose her mind. Instead of feeling better about herself, she had become severely depressed and was on the brink of insanity.

Ann and I chatted a few moments about the positive benefits of a deep relationship with God as the source of strength, confidence and success in life. Immediately, she began to dig in and learn about who God was and how she could know him better. Today Ann has a deep relationship with God, and he has blessed her with a successful business and healthy relationships with friends and family.

Susan, however, rebuffed Ann's biblically centered advice and went on to become "her own god," as she put it. She relied on herself and others to give her confidence and strength. As a result, Susan succeeded less and left in her wake a trail of broken people, broken relationships and broken promises.

It is possible to seek confidence and achievement by ourselves—at least symbols of achievement like titles, power, money and possessions—but miss inner contentment. And it is possible to have all the perks of achievement and feel great about ourselves—but we may be the only one who feels that way because we have used and stepped on people to get what we want out of life. When we try to take shortcuts in order to achieve instead of being confident in God to provide for and bless us, we live with the fear that one day the other shoe will drop, the skeleton will fall out of the closet, or our telltale heart will pound right out of our chest. Anything short of God's view on life, and we shortcut the very character we need to achieve. True achievement only exists when our confidence comes from God and our gain results from a life of integrity.

A godly woman with a heart of integrity not only has confidence, she inspires confidence.

The Rewards of Confidence

A godly woman with a heart of integrity not only has confidence, she inspires confidence. With that confidence comes achievement, not only in this world, but more important, in the one beyond where God has rewards waiting for us that will make any benefit package here on earth pale in comparison.

This book is dedicated to my friend Vyonda Benson, a woman who achieved with integrity and inspired with her achievement. Vyonda was a woman who survived the Depression, the Dust Bowl and many economic downturns. She married young, partly to escape a raging, violent father. She bore four children, and then suddenly her husband was diagnosed with crippling arthritis and was retired early by his company due to this disability. But because of her faith in God, Vyonda was confident that he would provide. With only a ninth grade education, Vyonda and her family started their own business.

Over the twelve years I knew Vyonda, I never heard her complain. She didn't complain about pain, trials, finances, people — she didn't complain. Instead Vyonda had a quiet confidence and a steady faith. She successfully sailed through some deep waters and storms because she knew God.

Just hours before her death, in a quiet moment in her bedroom, I picked up the frail body of my dear brave friend and held her so she could breathe just a bit better. I sang to her, hymns of the faith, knowing that she had achieved much here on earth but her best rewards were still ahead. I am convinced that as she stepped across eternity's threshold she heard, "Well done, my good and faithful servant."

Some motivational leaders say that the woman in the mirror is her own god, the master of her destiny. But I know all my imperfections and shortcomings. I am utterly human. I do not want to rely on my own strength and power. I want to rely on something—some one—who is all-powerful, all-knowing, all-loving. I want to achieve by seeing God clearly, through understanding his Word and through living life based upon that grand glimpse of the majestic.

Confidence Can Be Yours

It was one of those days. It must have been a Monday. I had been away at speaking engagements all weekend, and when I picked up the phone to listen to my messages, the automated voice blared in my ear, "You have thirty-one messages." I slammed down the receiver, and turned on my computer to retrieve my e-mail: "You've got mail! You've got mail! You've got mail!" I looked across my desk. Stacks of correspondence needed answers, and a half-written manuscript and research books created a tower of pressing priorities. I let out a long, frustrated sigh. I was officially overwhelmed.

I had made a previous commitment to God that I wouldn't start my work day unless I'd first spent time with him. And this day I'd jumped the gun.

I reached across my desk for my dog-eared copy of one of my favorite devotionals, *Daily Light for the Daily Path*, a book that gathers verses of the Bible together by topic into daily readings. The day was January 8, so I opened the book and read:

> I know whom I have believed and am persuaded that He is able. Able to do exceedingly abundantly above all that we ask or think. Able to make all grace abound toward you, that you, always having all sufficiency in all things, may have an abundance for every good work. Able to aid those who are tempted. Able to save to the uttermost those who come to God through Him, since He always lives to make intercession for them. Able to keep you from stumbling, and to present you faultless before the presence of His glory with exceeding joy. Able to keep what I have committed to Him until that day. Who will transform our lowly body that it may be conformed to His glorious body, according to the working by which He is able even to subdue

all things to Himself. "Do you believe I am able to do this?" They said to Him, "Yes, Lord." "According to your faith let it be to you."[9]

Able, able, able! I felt free to be me and let God be God. He was able. I didn't have to do it all and be it all—he could enable me to carry out that which he deemed vital from his perspective—and he'd help me be able to see exactly what that would be!

Being so encouraged by this devotional, I immediately thought of my other friends in various places of leadership who might also be encouraged by it. I opened up the devotional to copy it. I opened to January 8, and it wasn't there. I thought maybe I had mistakenly opened to February 8, but it wasn't there either. No, it was the March 8 devotional I had read. March 8! My God was so able that he led me to read the wrong date's reading on the right day for me. He is able!

You too will find that he is able, and with that knowledge, you will become a woman of confidence.

Winning Words

For you have been my hope, O Sovereign LORD, my confidence since my youth. I have no fear of sudden disaster or of the ruin that overtakes the wicked, for the LORD will be my confidence and will keep my foot from being snared. In him and through faith in him I may approach God with freedom and confidence. I am confident of this, that he who began a good work in me will carry it on to completion until the day of Christ Jesus, I will approach the throne of grace with confidence, so that I may receive mercy and find grace to help me in my time of need. This is the confidence I have in approaching God: that if I ask anything according to his will, he hears me. And if I know that he hears me — whatever I ask — I know that I have what I asked of him. I am confident of better things — things that accompany salvation. Therefore, brothers, since I have confidence to enter the Most Holy Place by the blood of Jesus, by a new and living way opened for me through the curtain, that is, his body, and since I have a great priest over the house of God, I will draw near to God with a sincere heart in full assurance of faith, having my heart sprinkled to cleanse me from a guilty conscience. . . . I will hold unswervingly to the hope I profess, for he who promised is faithful.[10]

Winning Ways

When are you least confident? For example, I used to lose confidence when I received a phone message from someone I deemed important. I used to go into a tailspin thinking I must have disappointed him or her in some way. This was totally an irrational thought linked back to being a child of an alcoholic father and never seeming to please him. As I studied God's character as a father, however, this unconfident behavior of not wanting to return phone calls that are the most important has nearly dissolved away.

What causes you to lose confidence? Your boss's look? Your spouse's response? New situations? The learning curve? A difficult person? Life not going your way?

Write a letter to God in your journal, naming the confidence robbers in your life and asking him to help you overcome them.

2

ℰPPORTUNITY

---

*"When one door of happiness closes, another opens:
but often we look so long at the closed door that we do not see
the one which has been opened for us."*
HELEN KELLER

he applause erupted! People were shouting, standing and whistling appreciation for the slim ballerina in white. But as they placed the crown upon her head, she couldn't hear the applause, or even the congratulations. Heather Whitestone, crowned Miss America in 1995, couldn't hear the well-wishing applause because she is deaf.

What most people don't realize is that the steps to that Miss America crown were long, painful and repeated. Many of us would never hang in there as first runner-up over and over again—especially when nearly everyone said Heather's dream would never be a reality.

The Lord of the Dance
When Heather was a toddler, her mother dropped a set of pans in the kitchen and realized that Heather could not hear. While other children played, Heather worked to learn to read lips and pronounce words correctly, but at family gatherings Heather would miss jokes and conversations.

Heather needed a haven. For a while, she attended a school for the deaf in St. Louis, far from her home in the South. But when she returned to public school from her school for the deaf, Heather felt alone. "My loneliness was eased, though, because at that time I discovered what it meant to have a personal relationship with Jesus Christ."[1]

Heather also found solace in dance. In early elementary school, frustrated with the inability to effectively communicate, she began ballet class, and in dance she discovered a safe emotional harbor. Heather explains her love of dance in the book *Listening with My Heart:*

> Dancing is a natural, expressive way to bring praise and glory to God. I had first come to this conclusion on Christmas Eve when I was very young. I waited until everyone in the house went to bed, then I slipped into the living room and turned on the Christmas tree lights. Caught by the wonder and the spirit of Christmas, I pretended to be the Virgin Mary. With a baby doll we used to represent the infant Jesus, I danced around the tree, offering my dance as a celebratory gift to God. It became my secret, personal tradition which I repeated every year, and I always felt that God enjoyed it tremendously.

Like most teens, Heather wanted to fit in, but she also wanted to be the best at something. "Because I wanted to have something special to show my children, I decided to enter my first pageant—the Shelby County Junior Miss program. Even though I didn't win—I was second runner-up—this was a great experience because it brought me out of my isolation and helped me relate to girls my own age."

Reaching for the Stars

Getting older didn't immediately erase Heather's longing to belong. In college she entered the Miss Deaf Alabama pageant. She hoped she would feel at home and fit right in. However, she soon realized that she had learned Exact Signed English, and everyone else, including the judges, was using American Sign Language.

> Over and over I prayed, "God, who am I? Hearing or deaf?" . . . Negative thoughts seemed to badger my every waking thought and moment. Vaclav Havel once said, "There are times when we must sink to the bottom of our misery to understand truth, just as we must descend to the bottom of a well to see the stars in broad daylight." . . . But God brought me back from the edge of despair by guiding my reading of the Bible. . . . By turning to

the comfort of my Bible, I came to rest in God's love for me. Though I still didn't know where I'd find a place in this world, I knew that I was in capable hands: God's.

Hearing God's voice in my heart and in his word began opening up the whole world to me. One night I looked up at the stars and noticed that all the stars looked different. Later I discovered that the Bible says that even the stars differ from each other in their beauty and brightness (1 Cor. 15:41). . . . That truth is so comforting! . . . God knows us better than we know ourselves. He knows our full potential, and he holds a bright, *realistic* dream for each one of us.

One evening during Heather's freshman year of college, Heather and her mother watched the Miss America pageant on TV. Heather was enthralled: "*The first*. The words sparked my imagination. I want to have that opportunity. . . . I want to perform my ballet on television."

Her mom's first response was to tally up the financial cost. Her mother took on a second job in addition to her teaching job, and during the year Heather actively competed she held down three jobs!

Heather competed in the Miss Alabama contest and only received first runner-up, but she won Miss JBU so she made plans to return to the Miss Alabama contest and committed herself to hours of studying, dancing rehearsal, community service and developing a platform.

Heading into her second Miss Alabama pageant, Heather was expected to win, and as the announcement came, Heather's name was announced as . . . first runner-up. Heather was astonished. "*No, not me!* As I walked to get my flowers and take the first runner-up position—for a second time—I thought, 'How can I do this? How can I come so close and not win? What is wrong with me?' "

Heather decided not to try for the title a third time. But then she received a letter that changed her mind:

I wanted you to know that a deaf man came to me looking for a job. . . . I didn't know whether or not I should hire him until I saw you on stage. I watched how you mastered your situation and overcame your problems. I really admired your efforts, and because of your example, I decided to hire the deaf man and give him a chance.

Heather reflects on that day, "Even if you think you will never reach your dream, remember that you will learn something and touch others on the journey."

Even if you think you will never reach your dream, remember that you will learn something and touch others on the journey. HEATHER WHITESTONE

Heather went back to work and developed her platform, the STARS program. She wanted to help children develop a positive attitude and reach for the stars!

As she headed for the Miss Alabama contest one last time, a friend, Teresa Strickland, who helped coach and encourage Heather, dropped her a note:

Heather, stay focused on Jesus. When you're competing in the pageant, keep your focus on him. If you lose your focus, you will not get through the tough situations. So follow Jesus in your heart. Don't let gossip or the audience or a mistake you might make control you. Only Jesus. Let him rule your heart.

On the night of the contest, when the moment for the announcement of the winner arrived, Heather was on pins and needles. "At that moment I felt a sudden sinking feeling—almost like a kid who has to welcome a new baby sister but feels that somehow she's been displaced. Then the girl next to me grabbed my hand. . . . *Dear God, tell me what is going on?* The audience went wild. I couldn't hear the name, but the girl next to me turned and said, "You won. Heather, you won!"

Honor Brings Responsibility
Months later when Heather arrived in Atlantic City for the Miss America pageant, the voice in her heart said, *Don't worry, Heather, I'm in charge. Relax. Dance for me.*

So she rested in the person of Christ—and all America watched in awe at the sight of a beautiful woman, a woman who couldn't hear a note, dance flawlessly to the accompanying music. As she danced, Heather depicted the steps to the cross that her Savior took: Jesus displaying his love with each step, Heather displaying her appreciation of his work in her life with each of her steps.

Finally, it was time for the final announcement, and again Heather couldn't hear it. But she could see someone point to her, and she could feel the crown being pinned to her head. As she walked the stage she waved to the crowd and gave everyone watching the "I love you" sign.

But the crown didn't remove the obstacles—it provided new ones—and new opportunities. Heather was swept away into a relentless schedule, had limited privacy and was engaged in controversy over lip reading and sign language, yet she kept listening to the voice in her heart, the voice of God.

One day, exhausted, in yet one more airport waiting for another late airplane, Heather saw a woman and her daughter coming toward her. They were also waiting for the delayed plane. The little girl, ill and sitting in a wheelchair, recognized Heather. Heather, moved by the little girl, took her crown out of its small wooden carrying case and placed it upon the little girl's head. A small gesture. A small act of kindness.

Two years later Heather was handed a large check in an elaborate ceremony by CEO Elmer Harris. It seems that a corporate executive from his company had witnessed the scene in the airport and had been moved to tears, and moved to tell the story to his company CEO. The Heather Whitestone Foundation was launched, and its purpose? To help others reach their dreams!

Finding the Silver Lining

Thomas Edison once said, "Opportunity is missed by most people because it is dressed in overalls and looks like work."[2] The hardest work is often trying to find the silver lining in a tough situation. Heather Whitestone faced some very tough situations in her life, but she also trusted in God to guide her to the opportunities awaiting her.

Finding the silver lining isn't hard for God. In fact, he promises to create silver linings out of nothing! Romans 8:28 and 31 say it best, "And we know that in all things God works for the good of those who love him, who have been called according to his purpose. . . .What, then, shall we say in response to this? If God is for us, who can be against us?"

God is the master of taking dark and turning it into light; taking bad
and bending it into good; taking seeming misfortune and making it into
fortunate opportunity. Writer Chuck Swindoll says that "we are all faced
with a series of great opportunities that are often brilliantly disguised as
impossible situations."[3]

So how do you look for the silver lining? I try to take a step-by-step
approach.

Tell the truth. I start with admitting that the situation looks bad. But I
also know that God is good. I usually throw in a verse or two that I've
memorized from the Bible, like Psalm 84:11: "No good thing does the
LORD withhold / from those who walk uprightly" (NRSV).

---

*When we walk to the edge of all the light we have and step out into the dark-
ness of the unknown, we must believe that there will be something solid to
stand on or that we will be taught how to fly!*

Rest in God's character. I make myself set my tears and feelings aside for a
moment, walk myself straight into God's throne room and take a good
hard look at his character. Then I say what I know to be true from the
Bible. God is good, God is all-knowing, God is all-powerful, God sees
everything and so on.

By resting in the character of God, you gain a new perspective and a
personal peace. One of Heather Whitestone's favorite quotes is, "When we
walk to the edge of all the light we have and step out into the darkness of
the unknown, we must believe that there will be something solid to stand on
or that we will be taught how to fly!" I wonder how high we could soar, if
we would only choose to step out in peace, resting in the person of God.

No obstacle is too big for God to overcome. Nothing can stop his plan.

Ah, Sovereign LORD, you have made the heavens and the earth by your
great power and outstretched arm. Nothing is too hard for you. (Jer
32:17)

He does as he pleases with the powers of heaven and the peoples of the
earth. No one can hold back his hand or say to him: "What have you
done?" (Dan 4:35)

For nothing is impossible with God. (Lk 1:37)

I am the vine; you are the branches. If a man remains in me and I in him, he will bear much fruit; apart from me you can do nothing. (Jn 15:5)

The LORD Almighty has sworn, "Surely, as I have planned, so it will be, and as I have purposed, so it will stand." . . . For the LORD Almighty has purposed, and who can thwart him? His hand is stretched out, and who can turn it back? (Is 14:24, 27)

Remember the former things, those of long ago;
    I am God, and there is no other;
    I am God, and there is none like me.
I make known the end from the beginning,
    from ancient times, what is still to come.
I say: My purpose will stand,
    and I will do all that I please.
From the east I summon a bird of prey;
    from a far-off land, a man to fulfill my purpose.
What I have said, that will I bring about;
    what I have planned, that will I do. (Is 46:9-11)

Heather rested in God's character and danced into her own dream, and now she is helping others dance into their dreams too. Let God's winning words give you the confidence to dance into your dreams.

Winning Words

I am able to do immeasurably more than all you ask or imagine, according to my power that is at work within you. Mine is the greatness and the power and the glory and the majesty and the splendor, for everything in heaven and earth is mine. Mine is the kingdom; I am exalted as head over all. Wealth and honor come from me; I am the ruler of all things. In your hands are strength and power to exalt and give strength to all. I am beyond your reach and exalted in power; in my justice and great righteousness, I do not oppress. I, the Sovereign LORD, come with power, and my arm rules for me. See, my reward is with me, and my recompense accompanies me. I give strength to the weary and increase the power of the weak. I, the Sovereign LORD, have made the heavens and the earth by my great power and outstretched arm. Nothing is too hard for Me. I rescue and save. May the God of hope fill you with all joy and peace as you trust in him, so that you may overflow with hope by the power of the Holy Spirit.[4]

Winning Ways

What circumstance seems impossible in your life? Are you tired of trying? Tired of striving?

Heather had people in her life who continually told her positive truth. Who tells you the truth about yourself and the truth about God and his strength and power? When things get really tough, ask your friends, family or small group to tell you positive truth. Or maybe you know someone who is discouraged and feels like giving up. Bombard their life with truth: send e-mails, faxes, letters, cards, voicemail messages—all filled with positive truth. When I come across a verse that proclaims God's awesome power, I copy it on to a brightly colored note card and post it on my bathroom mirror so I can read the verse day in and day out until I have it memorized. Or begin your own "Promises of God" journal where you write verses that have given you courage or strength to go forward in life. Then when things get tough, you will have verses handy that can encourage you to dance into your dream!

3

$\mathscr{P}$RIORITIES

"How we leave the world is more important than how we enter it."
JANETTE OKE

$\mathscr{W}$ho is more successful: the woman who climbs the ladder to the top, or the one holding the ladder for others?

I sat listening in admiration. I had just finished giving my speech, and the woman sitting next to me was going to the lectern next. As the emcee read my colleague's introduction, I thought, *Whew! I'm glad I went first!* Her bio listed so many accomplishments that I felt exhausted. She had a Ph.D., was chair of her department, had been selected twice for Outstanding Young Woman in America, and had received the Outstanding Faculty Award three times. She was a member of the local school board, and numerous professional groups had awarded her for her community service. She was a national writer, speaker and talk show host, and she was happily married with two great kids! She had made it to the top!

But when Dr. Shirley Weber began to speak, I saw just how long the road to success had been for her.

She was born the sixth of eight children in Hope, Arkansas, to sharecroppers. Her family had mastered the art of doing without. When she was a college student struggling to make it financially, she would come to church each week, and one elderly woman would tuck a dollar in her hand. The next week another would hand her a five. When she would get discouraged at the workload, it was those dear older women in her church who would encourage her. "You can do it! Hang in there!" they would echo in a chorus as lively and determined as the music they sang in church.

Many of these older women worked as housekeepers for the rich families in Westwood, home to the college Shirley attended, UCLA. Shirley knew their days consisted of getting up early and taking the bus from the gang-ridden projects in East Los Angeles to ritzy Westwood. In Westwood, these women would cook and care for other people's children, then take the long bus ride back home to East Los Angeles where they would cook and care for their own children. These women fought to keep their children safe, fed and educated day in and day out.

Many others who would tuck money into Shirley's hand worked as scrubwomen. While driving to UCLA she would see these women, carrying bags in each hand up the hill to the university, their ankles swollen from years and years of hard work. Often Shirley would stop her tiny, beat-up car and offer to drive the women up the hill.

When Shirley got discouraged, thinking life was hard for her, she would look at those dear women, trudging up that hill day in and day out. Dr. Weber, with tears brimming in her eyes and emotion in her voice declared with triumph: "Those women carried me up the hill to my education!"[1]

Yes, those women banded together, all with the priority of creating a future for a young woman who could help create a future for many— their children and grandchildren! Their sacrifice and love paid off. Today Dr. Weber is a role model of hope to thousands of inner-city women. Dr. Weber is committed to helping others gain a step up in life through learning. She has dedicated her life to education as a professor, school board member and talk-show host, and has received the Living Legacy award given by the Women's International Center for contributions in education, justice and humanity.

Reflecting God's Generosity

Oseola McCarty, a quiet woman who was forced to quit school in sixth grade to care for an ill relative, spent a lifetime ironing and washing other people's clothing. She went about her work with a godly attitude and made serving the Lord her number one priority. In her book *Simple Wisdom,* Oseola writes:

> I knew there were people who didn't have to work as hard as I did, but it didn't make me feel sad. . . . I never felt helpless. I always knew that thanks to my health and strength I could do for myself and make a way. Give me some work to do and I can make it. We are responsible for the way we use our time on this earth, so I try to be a good steward. I start each day on my knees, saying the Lord's Prayer. Then I get busy about my work. I get to cleaning or washing. I find that my life and my work are increasing all the time. I am blessed beyond what I hoped.[2]

When Oseola began her worklife at twelve years of age, her fee for washing a bundle of clothes was a mere $1.50 per bundle, yet by the time she retired at age 86 because of arthritis, she had managed to save $280,000. But instead of thinking of how she could spend the money on herself, Oseola donated $150,000 in scholarship money to the University of Mississippi because she wanted to help "somebody's child go to college."

My only regret is that I didn't have more to give. OSEOLA MCCARTY

As a follower of Jesus, Oseola always made it a priority to help others, even when she didn't have much herself: "What I know about Jesus is that there was nothing but love in Him. Even when they nailed His hands and feet, He was loving. It helps to think about that when going through hard times."

Oseola offers this practical advice on choosing priorities in life: "I think the way we live matters, not for now but for always. There's an eternal side to everything you do." She explains:

> When I leave this world, I can't take nothing away from here. I'm old and I won't live always—that's why I gave the money to the school and put my affairs in order. I planned it and I am proud of it. I am proud that I worked hard and that my money will help young people who have worked hard to deserve it. I'm proud that I am leaving something positive in this world. My only regret is that I didn't have more to give.

One Wednesday afternoon, a teenager answered the phone and heard some very good news. She, Stephanie Bullock, would be the first recipient of the Oseola McCarty scholarship fund. Stephanie was president of her high school and had served as a class officer each year in high school. She was a member of the National Honor Society, Beta Club, the mayor's appointee to the city's youth council and an active member of her Baptist church—and she was from a low-income family with a twin brother also headed for college. The thought of what that was going to do to the family budget weighed heavy on Stephanie's heart. But Stephanie's need was met by a woman with priorities beyond herself, a woman who never reached the top educationally herself but who was a success in her highest goal—holding the ladder for others.

Setting Priorities

In a world with constantly changing values, how does one decide how to set priorities? What priorities have timeless value and reap eternal rewards? The answer requires us to study the character of God. Who is he? What are *his* priorities?

Internal over external. God cares about our internal emotional and spiritual needs. We can easily get wrapped up in wanting to achieve success according to the world's standards. But God's priority is my internal spiritual life, so my priority should be to nurture my internal character. First Samuel 16:7 says, "Man looks at the outward appearance, but the LORD looks at the heart." So I try to keep matters of the heart a higher priority too.

Recently my oldest son, Brock, reminded me of the importance of living with integrity even when no one is looking. Brock is the starting quarterback for his football team, and he always chooses to stay late and help the coaches put away equipment or encourage teammates who might have to do extra laps. One night I had to pick up Brock and then take him home before going to a Bible study I was supposed to lead. I was in a hurry, and as usual, when I arrived, only Brock remained on the field, putting equipment away. It was dark, cold and lonely on the field. Even the coaches had disappeared.

"Brock, hurry! I need to go!" I shouted.

"Just a minute, Mom," Brock said as he wearily walked toward me. "I can't go quite yet. See, the coach said if we hadn't sent our beg letter, we have to do 10 repos." (Beg letters are fundraising letters, and repos are exercises where the athlete must run ten yards down the field, stop and do a push-up and repeat it all the way up and down the field. Repos are *hard* work.)

My schedule had just been thrown off—way off. For a moment I thought, *No one is here. Brock always stays late to help. Isn't that repo enough? The coaches will never know, but* . . . the Holy Spirit stopped me . . . *but God and Brock will know.*

"Okay, honey. And Brock, I'm proud of you for sticking to your word. It would be easy to walk away right now but—"

"But character counts, Mom."

Yes, character counts, I thought as I smiled, watching my son run and run and run.

Concentrating on developing your internal character instead of worrying about what others think of you is a priority that pays off. It's tempting to cut corners, but in the end, the difference between success and mediocrity is what we do when no one is watching—no one except God, that is.

It's tempting to cut corners, but in the end, the difference between success and mediocrity is what we do when no one is watching.

Holy over harried. God is a God of order. In his letter to the Corinthians, Paul writes, "For God is not a God of disorder but of peace" (1 Cor 14:33). I have usually found that in the hurry of rapid-fire decision making I can easily fall into an integrity lapse just because I haven't taken time to think things through.

If I am feeling pressured to decide in a difficult area or pressured to take a risk when I haven't had the opportunity to think it through, I can face some stiff consequences. Because I did not slow down to consider my actions, I have made poor investments, taken shortcuts on a project and placed my children in an awkward position.

Too often, we think we need to run ahead of God, help him out and fix a situation that seems to be in limbo. In the book of Genesis we read that

Abraham and his wife Sarah tried to do just that. Abraham and Sarah had no children, which was considered the ultimate failure in their culture. Neither of them was getting any younger, so Abraham and Sarah decided to take things into their own hands instead of waiting on God to bless them with an heir. Abraham slept with his Sarah's maid, and a son was born out of that liaison. Shortly afterwards Sarah found out she was pregnant, and she too bore a son. The conflict between those two sons has been passed down from generation to generation.

While it is important to be decisive, I have learned to slow down and weigh the consequences of my decision. If there is a check in my spirit, I need to investigate why it is there. If I am simply fearful about the situation, God will encourage my heart, but if I still have a deep sense of dread, I make it a priority to slow down and consider what is right.

People over product. People matter to God. We matter so much to him that he sent his son Jesus to die on the cross for our imperfections so we could be saved from ourselves. Jesus took physical beatings, emotional abuse, the mocking, the cruel remarks, the kangaroo court of injustice — he took it out of love for you and me. Even when Jesus was on the cross, his body racked with pain, his heart was overwhelmed with love for others. Looking down from the cross, he saw his mother, and knowing she would need someone to provide for her, Jesus told his disciple John to care for her.

I want to follow God's example and choose people over my own agenda, over material goods and over my personal comfort or gain.

I want to follow God's example and choose people over my own agenda, over material goods and over my personal comfort or gain. In my life, this may mean inviting a distraught friend in for coffee even if I'm on writing deadline, listening to a junior high girl with a broken heart without looking at my watch, or inviting the waiter who recognizes Bill and me to sit down and pour out *his* problemed love life over *our* romantic dinner.

Whatever the sacrifice, I want to follow the example of the women in this chapter, who saw to other's needs before their own, who gave generously, loved unconditionally and held the ladder for others to climb. May you, too, seek to make it a priority to place people over projects, eternal over immediate and the Holy Spirit's gentle whisper over a to-do list.

Winning Words

I made everything beautiful in its time. I also set eternity in the hearts of men; yet they cannot fathom what I have done from the beginning to the end. I am the Alpha and the Omega, the Beginning and the End. As the heavens are higher than the earth, so are my ways higher than your ways and my thoughts than your thoughts. Do nothing out of selfish ambition or vain conceit, but in humility consider others better than yourselves. Each of you should look not only to your own interest, but also to the interests of others. Your attitude should be the same as that of Christ Jesus. For he chose us in him before the creation of the world to be holy and blameless in his sight . . . for it is written: "Be holy, because I am holy." [3]

Winning Ways

What are the priorities in your life? Are you tempted to cut corners when no one is looking? Do you sense that your desire to achieve might be affecting the way you interact with people? Would others say that you treat them the same as Jesus would treat them if he were in your place? Is there a ladder you can hold for someone else today to help ensure they are a success? Is there something you can do today to give someone a step up in this world? Today when you face a decision, ask yourself: What would the character of God do in this situation?

4

$\mathscr{F}$AILURE

"It's never too late to be what you might have been."
GEORGE ELIOT

$\mathscr{H}$er name was in the headlines daily, her photo plastered in every paper and on the cover of nearly every magazine. Her name was a household word. Every tabloid maliciously labeled her: Donna Rice, the vixen who sidetracked Gary Hart's bid for the presidency.

How could a nice Christian girl, raised in a conservative churchgoing family, end up so off track?

After graduating from college in 1980, Donna won the title of Miss South Carolina World, and she headed to New York City to compete for the national title. After the pageant, she decided to stay in New York to try to launch her acting career, but she soon decided to move to Miami where she began a successful career as a television commercial actress — or so she thought.

One night, while with friends, Donna met Senator Gary Hart at a fundraiser. The party was so crowded that a small group, including Donna, went outside and on to a yacht owned by the resort's owner. After boarding, the group discovered that the boat was chartered by Senator Hart and some of his friends. Realizing their mistake, the group apologized and turned to leave — but they were invited to stay. As Donna was leaving the yacht later that night, Senator Hart asked for her phone number, and the next day, she and a friend were invited out for an afternoon on the ocean.

"Gary was the one who swept me off my feet. Before the boat docked, however, he confessed that because he was contemplating running for president, he couldn't separate from his wife. I believed him when he told me he faced a difficult choice between pursuing personal happiness and his political destiny.

"After he left Miami, he called me regularly. Two weeks later, he announced in a press conference he was running for president. When Gary continued to call, I became confused about his true feelings for me—and my own.

"One night, I flipped on the television and began watching the movie *Jesus of Nazareth*. Suddenly I was struck with how far off course I'd gotten, and I knew I couldn't continue with my current lifestyle. So on May 1, 1987, at Gary's invitation, I agreed to see him one last time—to confront him face to face about his sincerity and with the intention of ending our brief relationship. I didn't know I was walking into a trap—that reporters had been tipped off to stake out his house."[1]

Months later during a *20/20* interview, Donna finally put the pieces together. A friend of Donna's had taken pictures of Donna and Gary aboard ship. The "friend" had tried to sell the photos to the press, but the press demanded a story, so Donna was set up so that events could unfold before the watchful eyes of the press, who wanted to get a story about Senator Hart, the "womanizer." Soon Donna saw photos of herself plastered in the tabloids and whispered over in the coffee-break rooms around the world. She was center stage in the scandal of the presidential political election. Donna was shocked and devastated. She felt trapped and hopeless; her life was falling apart.

Same Song, Second Verse
Roll the hands of time back, and history provides abundant examples of women with destroyed reputations. Rahab was such a woman. People mocked her, whispered behind her back, laughed—but the men kept coming back. She was very good at what she did, and her family depended on her to provide—even if it was through prostitution.

One day some strangers came to town, and like most out-of-towners, they ended up at her house. But these men were different. They didn't want to use her. In fact, they extended a compassionate glance, a kind word, and instead of bringing pain they brought peace. Even though these men were spies, Rahab agreed to hide them in her home, and she boldly asked them to protect her family when the Israelites marched against Jericho:

> Before the spies lay down for the night, she went up on the roof and said to them, "I know that the LORD has given this land to you and that a great fear of you has fallen on us, so that all who live in this country are melting in fear because of you. . . . Now then, please swear to me by the LORD that you will show kindness to my family, because I have shown kindness to you. Give me a sure sign that you will spare the lives of my father and mother, my brothers and sisters, and all who belong to them, and that you will save us from death." . . .
>
> "Our lives for your lives!" the men assured her. "If you don't tell what we are doing, we will treat you kindly and faithfully when the LORD gives us the land."
>
> The men said to her, "This oath you made us swear will not be binding on us unless, when we enter the land, you have tied this scarlet cord in the window through which you let us down. . . . But if you tell what we are doing, we will be released from the oath you made us swear."
>
> "Agreed," she replied. "Let it be as you say." So she sent them away and they departed. And she tied the scarlet cord in the window. (Josh 2:3-21)

Days later, Rahab saw the Israelites marching toward Jericho. Her hope for a new life was in believing the stories of the men she'd hidden. *Could this God of theirs really be trusted? Is he just like the men I know—will he just use me and toss me aside, too? Or is he really as strong and powerful—and good—as I've heard in the rumors and from the lips of the Israelite spies?* Then she remembered the peace, the hope, the respect she had felt when the Israelite men came to her home. She wanted that hope every day for herself and her family, so she hung the scarlet cord out the window, praying, *God, please be who they say you are.*

Then the troops began to march. Day after day they marched. Finally, on the seventh day they drew their trumpets and the music blared—and the wall around Jericho fell, except for the place where the scarlet cord hung out the window. God was faithful—even to a hurting prostitute wishing for a fresh start.

A Cry for Mercy

Donna wished for a fresh start as well. The media feeding frenzy just worsened. She had to leave her job, and she couldn't stay anywhere longer than a week before the press found her. She wondered if she should speak out or keep silent as lies and half-truths were paraded before the public. She had no private life anymore. She had become the bimbo party poster girl. Like the walls of Jericho, her world seemed to be crumbling around her.

How did she pick herself up and go on when life seemed to just be headed for more and more pain? She called home and called out to God for mercy. Rahab cried out, Donna cried out, and all women looking for confidence cry out: *Please be who I know your Word says you are.*

God answered her cry for mercy and surrounded her with his love. Donna went to church and sobbed through the services. Her mother mailed her an audiotape from an old youth group friend that said, "Donna, I imagine you're in a lot of pain right now. I just want you to know God loves you and I love you." Christian friends formed a protective circle around her and helped her sort through media offers, book deals and phone calls. She found a new Christian roommate, and later at a prayer breakfast in Washington, D.C., she met some Christians who offered her a retreat, and for the next few months she rested there and gained renewed strength.

After the retreat, May Doremus, a leader of the prayer breakfast, offered Donna a safe place to stay, in her home with her husband and two children, and Donna accepted. At the time May was confined to a wheelchair and was a medical enigma. Donna felt like a social enigma, so the bond of friendship grew, as did Donna's relationship with God.

God walked Donna back through her life: In college she'd drifted and compromised her Christian values. She drank, partied and dated non-Christians. After graduation she dated an older guy, and one night after a few drinks, he forced her to have sex. Her virginity taken by a date rape, Donna felt afraid, ashamed and unloved.

The rape left her feeling like used goods, and she soon began a spiral downward into promiscuity. As her acting and modeling career took her upward to glitzy social circles, her heart was on a downward slope. It was at this time of inward turmoil that she had met Gary Hart and her life fell apart.

When we mess up, if we ask his forgiveness, He'll redeem those choices, using our mistakes as a "door of hope" for other people. DONNA RICE

Sorting through these old wounds, extending forgiveness to all those who had used her and accepting God's forgiveness for herself launched Donna forward again, forward on the path that God had for her. Over the next few years she climbed out of her depression. She began to read the Bible regularly, attend church and listen to Christian radio, and she surrounded herself with friends who wanted the best for her and would hold her accountable if she felt tempted to stray. Donna says:

> There are no easy answers, no quick solutions. But God is the great Restorer. In my case, I learned that although God loves us, he doesn't grant us immunity from the consequences of our choices. However, when we mess up, if we ask his forgiveness, He'll redeem those choices, using our mistakes as a "door of hope" for other people (Hos 2:14-15).

The Door of Hope
At times, I have felt like Donna and Rahab—in desperate need of mercy. Sometimes we set ourselves up for failure knowingly by poor choices, but sometimes our humanity and basic imperfection sets us up and all we can do is cry for mercy! Once, under a writing deadline, I missed an important detail. It was one that could have hurt someone who was already hurt by life's circumstances. It was a mistake that might have put the publishing house at risk legally, and I didn't catch it until a reader wrote and pointed it out. I was distraught. My failure could put so many I cared for in a bad place. There was nothing I could do except cry out to God for mercy and protection for all

involved and wait until it could be corrected in the next printing.

God longs to rescue us out of our trouble—even if we brought the calamity on by our own actions and decisions.

God longs to rescue us out of our trouble—even if we brought the calamity on by our own actions and decisions. He has the ability to restore us and redeem us—if we own up to our sin and we ask for mercy. When we leave our bargaining chips out of the deal and come to him, ready to leave our rebellious ways behind and seek his righteousness, we will find that God is full of mercy. All through the Bible we see evidence of this truth:

> The sacrifices of God are a broken spirit; a broken and contrite heart, O God, you will not despise. (Ps 51:17)

> Let the wicked forsake his way and the evil man his thoughts. Let him turn to the LORD, and he will have mercy on him, and to our God, for he will freely pardon. (Is 55:7)

> Blessed are the merciful, for they will be shown mercy. (Mt 5:7)

> But go and learn what this means: "I desire mercy, not sacrifice." For I have not come to call the righteous, but sinners. (Mt 9:13)

> Therefore, I urge you, brothers, in view of God's mercy, to offer your bodies as living sacrifices, holy and pleasing to God—this is your spiritual act of worship. (Rom 12:1)

> But for that very reason I was shown mercy so that in me, the worst of sinners, Christ Jesus might display his unlimited patience as an example for those who would believe on him and receive eternal life. (1 Tim 1:16)

Are you disappointed in the person you see in the mirror each morning? When people bring up conversations of standards, integrity and accountability, are you squeamish, afraid of being "found out"? Are you basically a good person, but one who has made some poor choices, lapsed in your judgment and are now waiting for the other shoe to drop? Don't wait for the other shoe to drop—run to God now and confess it all to Jesus. His mercy is freeing, his grace restoring. His death on the cross is your door of hope.

Donna walked through that door of hope and discovered that she could use her experiences to help others to find God's mercy and peace by working with the "Enough is Enough!" campaign, an organization that fights against pornography. "Because of my experiences, I have great empathy for victims of sexual abuse and pornography. Through 'Enough is Enough!' God is using what I've learned to impact other's lives and bring him glory. He's brought purpose to my pain—and he's thrown in some surprises, too, including my husband, Jack!" Donna married Jack in 1994, and now she's a mother, a wife and a successful advocate for God's standards.

The door of hope is open for you too. Step across God's threshold from failure to mercy.

Winning Words

O LORD, have mercy on me; heal me, for I have sinned against you. I am in deep distress. Let me fall into the hands of the LORD, for his mercy is great; but do not let me fall into the hands of men. In your great mercy you did not put an end to me or abandon me, for you are a gracious and merciful God. Remember me for this also, O my God, and show mercy to me according to your great love. Though I were innocent, I could not answer him; I could only plead with my Judge for mercy. In my alarm I said, "I am cut off from your sight!" Yet you heard my cry for mercy when I called to you for help. Do not withhold your mercy from me, O LORD; may your love and your truth always protect me. Have mercy on me, O God, according to your unfailing love; according to your great compassion blot out my transgressions. Have mercy on me, O God, have mercy on me, for in you my soul takes refuge. I will take refuge in the shadow of your wings until the disaster has passed. May your mercy come quickly to meet me, for I am in desperate need.

Have mercy on me, O LORD, for I call to you all day long. Turn to me and have mercy on me, as you always do to those who love your name. Have mercy on me, O LORD, have mercy on me, for we have endured much contempt. And forgive me, who has sinned against you; forgive all the offenses I have committed against you, and cause my conquerors to show me mercy. O LORD, hear my prayer; listen to my cry for mercy; in your faithfulness and righteousness come to my relief.

Who is a God like you, who pardons sin and forgives the transgression of the remnant of his inheritance? You do not stay angry forever but delight to show mercy. Your mercy extends to those who fear you, from generation to generation.

The wisdom that comes from heaven is first of all pure; then peace-loving, considerate, submissive, full of mercy and good fruit, impartial and sincere. Let us then approach the throne of grace with confidence, so that we may receive mercy and find grace to help us in our time of need. Praise be to the God and Father of our Lord Jesus Christ! In his great mercy he has given us new birth into a living hope through the resurrection of Jesus Christ from the dead. Mercy triumphs over judgment![2]

Winning Ways

Have you ever had to face up to a failure, the shame of poor decisions or the humiliation of shortsighted thinking? To whom did you turn to pour out your feelings of embarrassment and disgrace? Where did you go to feel safe enough to start again?

God wants to extend mercy to us when we fail. He has set a process in place to move us from a broken place to a better place.

Acknowledge God as the giver of grace. "And the LORD said, 'I will cause all my goodness to pass in front of you, and I will proclaim my name, the LORD, in your presence. I will have mercy on whom I will have mercy, and I will have compassion on whom I will have compassion'" (Ex 33:19).

Acknowledge your sin (the mistake, the wrong choice, rebellious act or attitude). "He who conceals his sins does not prosper, but whoever confesses and renounces them finds mercy" (Prov 28:13). Don't make excuses or rationalize—confess.

Amend your mistakes as much as possible. If you hurt another, apologize. If you can correct the mistake, then do so. If you can make amends, try to restore the relationship from your side. You may find new allies as you seek to make amends. To build a new life after a failure, you'll need a new support network to help you build new habits to replace old destructive ones. Replace old destructive thoughts and patterns by renewing your mind. Start with meditating and memorizing the winning words in this chapter.

Actively pursue accountability. Sin sneaks in. Read the appendix in this book and begin to pray about who you would like to be your "fine-tuning friends." Read and discuss this book together to lay a foundation for your friendship. Look at your schedule and create a weekly time for this level of friendship—a space for a walk, lunch, coffee or prayer.

5

$\mathscr{R}$ISK

---

*"One of the great advantages of getting older is knowing
more about what God means when he says,
'I'll work your life for good, if you let me have your life!'"*
STEPHANIE EDWARDS

$\mathscr{F}$or over eighteen years her beautiful face and perky greetings have welcomed in the New Year as millions tune into the Tournament of Roses parade. Stephanie Edwards is a broadcaster whose credits would fill this chapter. She has appeared on the Johnny Carson show fifteen times. She has hosted numerous television and radio programs, and for years she was the spokeswoman for the Lucky Supermarket chain, which earned her the nickname "The Luckiest Lady in Town."

If the truth be known, somewhere down in the recesses of our hearts, we all long for a moment of recognition of that magnitude—a moment that makes us feel like somebody special. But what most of us fail to see are the moments of risk and sacrifice that lead up to a moment like that. Even Stephanie Edwards has gone through moments of fear where she has had to take risks based on faith.

Stephanie and her husband, Murray MacLeod, were enjoying the fruits of years of successful work in both business and media when they decided to invest in some property in California. Shortly after, the bottom dropped out of the market, and they lost almost everything financially. Stephanie explains, "Financially speaking we will never recover.

But we have learned many things. We learned to love each other at our mutual worst. We also learned to be gracious, in knowing that most people think that we live on easy street."

Stephanie and Murray also learned to rely on God to see them through this difficult time, clinging to the truth of Romans 8:28: "And we know that in all things God works for the good of those who love him, who have been called according to his purpose." Stephanie says, "I know I am among legions of people who count on the fact that truly God causes even the worst things to work together for good. I am reminded as I grow older of the first half of the verse: he works all things together for those who love him who are called to *his* purpose. . . . I truly believe that we have learned a really blessed lesson about the fact that we must honor nothing except God's grace. Knowing God is the same, yesterday, today, tomorrow, has been the only constant. It has brought us closer to each other and to the Lord."

God is just as willing to bless the reader of this book as he is to bless the person that the reader admires most. STEPHANIE EDWARDS

The couple struggled about whether to keep their loss from the public eye or to share their experience with others: "We find ourselves on the one hand wanting to share our story by way of witness. However, on the other hand, if you tell the truth about having to start all over again, our industry does not admire that. In our industry, it is more admirable in ways to lose sobriety than to lose all your money."

In the end, they decided to tell their story, and Stephanie's willingness to risk sharing her own fears has produced an ever-increasing platform of influence as a broadcaster for L.A.'s largest Christian talk radio station. And in her thirty years of interviewing all kinds of successful people, she has learned that no one is immune to the fears and insecurities of risk: "Even those who seem supremely confident are covering insecurity, embarrassment, fear, and occasionally, self-loathing—and I mean *everybody*. I am convinced that underneath the shallow cosmetic surface by which we make so many erroneous judgments about each other, we are all exactly the same."

Stephanie also knows that if people go to God when they are hurting, he will bless us with his comforting presence. "God is just as willing to bless the reader of this book as he is to bless the person that the reader admires most. He's the same toward everyone in the way he is willing to bless. We need to know that and believe that."[1]

The Blessing of Brokenness

If we place our lives in God's hands, he promises to be with us when we encounter situations that involve great risk. Debra Maffit, crowned Miss America in 1983, has experienced God's faithfulness in her life on more than one occasion.

Debra had run for Miss Texas three times when a friend convinced her to come to California for a spot on a television show. After she arrived, the Miss California people encouraged her to run for Miss California.

> I had risked everything to come out to California. I had $300 to my name, and I knew if I didn't win the pageant, I couldn't get home. My parents didn't have the money to get me home. I had worked in a bakery to put myself through college and to pay for five years of pageants and voice lessons. I had gathered sponsors to help out along the way, and it really was blood, sweat and tears to get me to the pageant each time. But I borrowed $1,500 to get me through three months of living expenses and packed everything in my little beat-up car to get to Santa Cruz where the pageant was held.[2]

At the pageant, Debra was chosen as one of the ten finalists, but she felt like she had completely blown the talent portion.

> I felt that not only had I lost, I had lost embarrassingly. The orchestra leader had to signal the orchestra to stop. I wanted a crack in the stage to open up and the stage to swallow me. I wondered if they would let me start over for a moment, but I knew they wouldn't so I finished the song acappella, and I walked off the stage devastated. I could even hear some of the girls backstage cheering because I had blown it.

One godly older woman working backstage pulled Debra aside, offered up a quick prayer and said, "It's not over till it's over. You walk out there with your chin held high."

When the final contestants were called onto the stage for the naming of the winner, Debra was barely holding on to her composure.

> I was getting ready to lose it bad. I felt I was going to cry hard, so hard that it would have been embarrassing. I kept thinking about all those years of hard work, that because of my age, this was my last shot, that if I lost I had nowhere to go, nowhere to live, no money to return home. I thought about how I had lived my life, how I focused on *my* goals, *my* dreams. I had never stopped to ask God if these where his dreams for my life. At that moment I told God I was sorry, sorry I hadn't done life God's way.
>
> Then I realized those five years weren't wasted. I had learned so much. I prayed, *God, I didn't think of what you wanted, what you had for me. God, if you will just give me the strength to walk off this stage without losing it emotionally, I will be yours. I will go where you want me to go, do what you want me to do, be who you want me to be.* I think that was the first time I had ever really cried out to God. Instantly, I was flooded with peace. It was so awesome, so welcome. It no longer mattered to me if I won, I knew at that moment that God would watch over me and give me peace.
>
> Then they called out my name as Miss California. I cried for three straight days.

Debra had just a few short months to prepare for the Miss America pageant, and she was dreading the talent portion of the pageant, even though she heard that the tape of the talent portion had been edited. "I knew that same horrible fear that had caused me to blow my talent over and over was still there. I knew the fear hadn't been edited out." To make matters worse, the news of Debra's weakness traveled the pageant grapevine.

Debra bolstered her courage by seeking out God.

> Some precious prayer warriors involved in the California pageant took me to a little church and prayed over me. I started getting into God's Word and used it for prayer. I also got to talk to a former Miss America who had an inner strength, beauty, and confidence, and I asked her how she handled the talent section. She replied, "When I get up on stage, I pray that God would use me as a vessel to pour his love out to the audience." I realized then that my focus had been all wrong.

The day of the pageant arrived, and when it was time for Debra to perform, she faced an arena large enough to hold two football fields, and the stage was ten times larger than any she had ever performed on. She was petrified.

> I prayed my second prayer, crying out to God, *Please let me pour out your love.* I felt his presence so strong. I had so much peace, I had no fear. There was quietness, a peace, like I had been scooped up and set in a special quiet place. After I performed I knew I had performed better than I ever had and I knew I had supernatural help. I knew it didn't matter if I won. I had learned all I needed to learn. No matter what I had to face in life, I could turn to God and completely lean on his strength and ability and I could make it through anything.

Debra was crowned Miss America, and her life became a whirlwind of activity. She was booked in a different city every day. She was given two shows in Hollywood, and she was booked in and out of Las Vegas and on the speaking circuit. "I was working 24 hours a day 7 days a week," said Debra. "I was hosting multiple shows. One week, I'd be on 'Hollywood Squares,' the next week I'd be doing a show with Regis."

Amidst all her success, Debra felt like something was missing. She would read her Bible in hotels room, but she wasn't able to regularly attend church. She fellowshipped and prayed everywhere she could but she felt as if she was caught up in the fast track and life was carrying her along at breathtaking speed.

> Without the support of a home church or a group and Christians for support, I couldn't sustain my walk. I didn't have the wisdom to know I needed to be in the Word every day and in a supportive local church. I had a heart for God, but . . . I remember I went to New York on a date, we were eating at one of the fanciest hotels, I was wearing an expensive gown, he was driving an expensive car, but I remember being so unhappy, feeling so empty. I turned my back and covered my face so my date couldn't see my tears. I remember thinking, *If this is all life has to give, it's not enough to live for. If this is it, I don't want to live.*

Shortly thereafter, Debra met another Miss America, Dr. Shirley Cothrin, and God spoke to Dr. Cothrin's heart on Debra's behalf: *It is not what it seems. Debra is unhappy, pray for her.*

Debra explains, "I had left God, but God hadn't left me. Because his spirit was in me, there was only one place of peace and joy, with him." Debra watched as God took her out of the limelight and fast lane and brought her to a place she could think again.

> God proceeded to take all the things away from me, and he brought me back. He gave me a hunger for his Word and his presence. He plugged me into a local church and filled me with his spirit. He gave me a wonderful husband and two wonderful children. Before, I had money and possessions, but I had no life and no love.

When we lean on our strength, we cut off God's power, but when we enter into his rest and cling to Christ, all of who he is can flow through us. DEBRA MAFFIT

Today Debra has an active life. She still hosts television shows and makes media appearances, but she also enjoys her family, her church and the simple things of life. When I appeared on a television show she was hosting, I caught a glimpse of the new strength and confidence that Debra lives out on a daily basis—and the source of that confidence: "I learned to embrace trial and learned to praise God in the valley, because when you're there God pulls back the veil and you get a bigger picture. When we lean on our strength, we cut off God's power, but when we enter into his rest and cling to Christ, all of who he is can flow through us."

From Heartbreak to Hollywood

She didn't want it, she tried to stop it, but the event Holly McClure most feared—divorce—was thrust upon her.

> When I was going through my divorce, life looked bleak and depressing for me. Many times I would have one of those days when I would have given up if somebody would have let me. I was sinking into a deep depression about the loss of my marriage, my life and what I was going to do with it. I had no idea what direction I needed to take in the job market and what

kind of job I could get that would let me take care of my young children. Here I was, a single mother of three young children, depressed, hopeless.[5]

During the time of her divorce, Holly was living in California, and she lived for phone calls from family back in Texas. One day Holly's younger sister, Kelly, called and urged her to read Jeremiah 29:11-14, "Holly, I believe God gave me this verse for you. I've read it many times before and I'm sure you have, but it's never jumped out at me like it did this time. When I was reading it, God told me this verse is for you!"

When Holly hung up, she read the passage:

"For I know the plans I have for you," declares the LORD, "plans to pros-per you and not harm you, plans to give you hope and a future. Then you will call upon me and come and pray to me and I will listen to you. You will seek me and find me when you seek me with all of your heart. I will be found by you," declares the LORD, "and will bring you back from captiv-ity. I will gather you from the places I have banished you and will bring you back from the place which I carried you into exile."

Holly wept, realizing how much God cared for her when seemingly no one else did. Day after day she read and re-read those verses, gaining strength from the promises in God's Word.

The hope that this verse gave to me was not only that God had a plan for my life, but that I had a future that he would take care of. I felt God was giving me explicit instruction to call upon him, pray to him, seek him with all of my heart and be found by him and be gathered from the place I was banished to (Irvine, California) and come out of my exile (divorce).

Even though it took me a while to get emotionally healthy and process through my pain from divorce, the hopelessness lifted because I *knew* I had a father, husband, friend, counselor, lover-of-my-soul God who would never leave me, forsake me or abandon me. I knew he would take care of me and had a plan for my life even though I had no idea what it was.

I was a new creature with a hope and a plan. I became intimate with him and learned to trust in him as I had trusted in no man before. I began to understand and learn about his loving and forgiving nature, and that no matter what I did, he would still love me!

Banking on God's loving nature became a lifeline for Holly. When her ex-husband took her to court to reduce her child support and she was ordered by a judge to put her children in childcare and find a job, she cried out to God, "Lord, what should I do?"

Holly felt God clearly leading her: *Stick with what you know.* "That wasn't exactly the long explanation that I wanted so I stubbornly asked him again: What can I do, Lord? What can I do that will make a difference and will be in your will? What do *you* want me to with the talents you gave me?"

God repeated his instruction: *Stick with what you know, Holly, and I will make it enough. I will set you before kings and high places and you will have favor with many. I will take care of your career. Just do what I give you to do, and I'll do the rest.*

Holly had done radio and television commercials and written a movie review column when she lived in Albuquerque, but that had been a long time ago. Now Holly was facing her future, and she needed to make a move, so she put her trust in God and decided to pursue a career in writing movie reviews to help parents discern what movies would be appropriate for themselves and their children. She wrote a column for some small newspapers until it was picked up by the *Orange County Register.* Within six months, her column was syndicated across the country in over three hundred newspapers. One year later, Holly's column was noticed by a morning radio talk show, and she was asked to talk about her reviews on air.

God can take whatever your talents are and use them to further his kingdom and you. HOLLY MCCLURE

Holly's career blossomed. She became a regular on one of L.A.'s largest stations, KKLA, and hosted her own movie review show called *Holly on Hollywood.* She appeared as a guest on numerous television shows, including *Montel Williams, Politically Incorrect* and *The Charles Grodin Show.*

Today, Holly is a talk show host for KPRZ in San Diego where she's heard daily on *Holly McClure Live* and Saturdays on *Holly on Hollywood.* She does weekly television reviews on Orange County News Network as well as her weekly column in the paper. She has successfully maintained exposure in print, radio and television, and recently she was asked to write movie reviews for Crosswalk.com. Holly is also a frequent public speaker for singles and women's groups.

Holly gives all the credit to God.

It's all because I listened to God and went with what I knew and let God do the rest. I'm in a tough business that relies on looks, age and who you know. But God continues to amaze me by bringing new experiences and ways to further my career. No matter what you look like, how old you are, where you live or how much money you don't have, God can take whatever your talents are and use them to further his kingdom and you! God can advance you in a career that you might think (at first) is impossible, but the key to getting there is letting God be in control. When God is advancing you, setting you before kings and high places and giving you favor, nothing else can compare to that feeling or rush you get knowing you are in his will.

God took a thirty-six year-old broken-hearted, wounded vessel with three young children, loved me, mended me, restored my soul and then set me on a journey I never would have dreamed possible. I could never have dreamed big enough for what God's done in my life. Each day I look forward with joy and anticipation for the new and incredible things that God is going to continue to bring my way.

A Future and a Hope
All the women in this chapter have discovered that life does not come without risk. But they each have a stability that gives them an edge—a God who doesn't change, doesn't shift, isn't fickle or flighty—but is solid as a rock. They have all discovered that risks based upon faith, scary steps of God's calling, always lead to stability.

Like Stephanie, Holly and Debra, I too find the only way I can risk and step onto the high wire of a new challenge or opportunity is to rely on God, who stands underneath us like a safety net. For you as well, he is changeless, secure and always there for you when you cry out to him.

Winning Words
Now to him who is able to do immeasurably more than all we ask or imagine, according to his power that is at work within us, . . . being confident of this, that he who began a good work in you will carry it on to completion until the day of Christ Jesus. God, who has called you into fellowship with his Son Jesus Christ our Lord,

is faithful. Every good and perfect gift is from above, coming down from the Father of the heavenly lights.

Teach me your way, O LORD; lead me in a straight path because of my oppressors.

Since you are my rock and my fortress, for the sake of your name lead and guide me. Teach me to do your will, for you are my God; may your good Spirit lead me on level ground. I, the LORD, guide you in the way of wisdom and lead you along straight paths. I will lead the blind by ways they have not known, along unfamiliar paths I will guide them; I will turn the darkness into light before them and make the rough places smooth. These are the things I will do; I will not forsake them. Whether you turn to the right or to the left, your ears will hear a voice behind you, saying, "This is the way; walk in it."[4]

Winning Ways

Have you cried out to God from a broken place? Are you still trying to manipulate circumstances and people to get what you want out of life or have you come to the place of having a heart of faith and trust? Place your dreams before God and ask God to prepare you to be the kind of person who could walk in those dreams if he wills them for you. A woman can achieve with integrity if she knows it is "'Not by might nor by power, but by my Spirit,' says the LORD Almighty" (Zech 4:6).

In your journal, write out those big dreams and the character qualities that you would need in order to carry out those dreams in a way that would give glory to God and grace to the people around you.

Study God's Word. I have seen in my role as a leader in ministry, that the more women study, memorize and meditate on the Bible and the more they have stood on the promise of God, the more they can risk with God. When I come to a fork in the road and I am seeking God's direction, I ask God to give me a verse to lead me to the next step. Then, I record that verse in the flyleaf of my Bible so that when things get tough, when criticism hits, when doubts assail me or when circumstances are difficult, I can go back to the Bible and remind myself of God's calling in my life. Instead of doubting my call, I can retune my ear to God's voice and wait for his new plan or ask him to show me his purpose. Today, write one verse, a few "winning words," in the flyleaf of your Bible to remind you of God's plan for your life.

Now take one more step. Tell someone, someone you trust, your hopes and dreams and ask them to pray with you.

6

$\mathscr{C}$LARITY

"Women are the real architects of society."
HARRIET BEECHER STOWE

$\mathscr{S}$lavery had etched itself into Harriet's heart. She knew that it was wrong, and she had an overwhelming desire to help those who were caught in the brutality of the world of slavery. She became active in the Underground Railroad and helped smuggle many slaves to safety and freedom. Once she even borrowed money to buy back a Negro child who had been sold to a different master than his mother. But Harriet longed to do more, something that would change hearts and save lives. But what could one woman possibly do?

One day while she was praying in church, Harriet encountered God's holiness, and suddenly her purpose was clear. In a daydream, she saw the characters and plot line of a story unroll before her. Inspired to obey the dream, Harriet Beecher Stowe, a young pastor's wife with six children, began to write the story in installments, finding time between her numerous other responsibilities. A small anti-slavery journal published her pieces, and over a year after she started, Harriet completed *Uncle Tom's Cabin.*

Even though the journal was originally a small publication, news of the compelling story traveled throughout the country—on both sides of the slavery issue. The publication hit the streets right after the 1850 Fugitive Slave

Law, a law which allowed slave owners to pursue runaway slaves even into free territory. Harriet caught the attention of the nation, the president and the world with a novel that humanized the plight of both the slave and slave owner, showing that the system abused everyone involved—the slave, the owner and the nation. The message spread like wildfire. The first day *Uncle Tom's Cabin* was released in book form, over three thousand were sold. Twenty thousand copies were sold in the next three weeks, and the book continued to draw recognition. Today, more than three million copies of the book have been distributed worldwide in twenty-two different languages.

Many admired Harriet's boldness in writing about such a controversial subject. In 1896, Charles Dudley Warner commented on *Uncle Tom's Cabin*, saying that Harriet "sought to light up the darkness."[1] Indeed, Harriet found clarity in her life when she embraced God's call to uphold justice and holiness, and when asked about the book, she would reply, "I did not write it. God wrote it. I merely did his dictation."[2]

God, the First Activist

Like millions of women, Harriet Beecher Stowe could have tried to dodge the heavy burden of trying to right the injustice of slavery. She might have used her financial woes as an excuse not to get involved. She consistently struggled to write enough to keep her and her pastor-professor husband and their family afloat. She could have used her family as a shield from responsibility as well. This mother of six in pre-Civil War times already had her hands full with domestic responsibilities. She could have used her talent for her own gain or glory, but she had encountered God's holiness, and with it came clarity.

Bing Hunter, author of *The God Who Hears*, describes God's moral purity in this way: "His inherent personal righteousness and holiness . . . is symbolized in Scripture as light: blinding, unending, undiminishing, dazzling whiteness."[3] So often we view justice, righteousness and holiness by our standards. Hunter brings the issue to our daily life:

> Another reason why holiness is so hard to understand is that Christians are like fish, living in a fluid medium (society) which has become so morally murky that "light" seems abnormal. We were born in dirty water and have gotten used to it. Mud and murk are normal; clean and light are threatening.

We can see rotten things on the bottom, but assume we cannot get stuck in the muck if we keep moving. And besides, we generally swim (in circles) higher up in the pond. We have learned to live comfortably with unholiness and see lots of others wearing Ichthus pins who do too. . . . It is little wonder sin grieves the Holy Spirit who lives in us (Eph 5:30). Yet the greater and more astounding wonder is that sin grieves us so little.[4]

The Bible explains that "everything that does not come from faith is sin" (Rom 14:23). Or as Hunter says, "Sin is the failure to live congruently with God's holiness."[5] Bill Bright, president and founder of Campus Crusade for Christ, points out the contrast between our sin and the holiness of God.

When I think of God's holiness, I am convicted by the sinful nature of my own being. We are all like a man wearing a beautiful white suit who was invited to go down into the depths of a coal mine. In the darkness of the mine, he was not aware that his suit was becoming soiled. But when he resurfaced into the dazzling light of the noonday sun, he was fully aware that his suit had become sooty and dirty. The light of God's holiness reveals the darkness of our sin.[6]

Nathan Stone, in his book *The Names of God*, states that *Jehovah M'Kaddesh* "means dedicate, consecrate, sanctuary, hallow, and holy and . . . it appears [in the Bible] in its various forms some 700 times. . . . It is of this holiness that an old Scottish divine writes: 'It is the balance . . . of all the attributes of Deity. Power without holiness would degenerate into cruelty; omniscience without holiness would become craft; justice without holiness would degenerate into revenge.'"[7]

What is the natural response when God reveals his holiness, his perfectly just and glorious character? Let's look at a few examples from people in the Bible who encountered the holiness of God.

Moses. When God revealed his glory to Moses atop Mt. Sinai, Moses was immediately inspired to obey God. Then he immediately wanted others to experience God:

Moses bowed to the ground at once and worshiped. "O Lord, if I have found favor in your eyes," he said, "then let the Lord go with us. Although this is a stiff-necked people, forgive our wickedness and our sin, and take us as your inheritance." (Ex 34:8-10)

Saul. Saul too came face to face with the glory of God on a trip to Damascus. As he neared Damascus, a light from heaven blinded him, and he fell to the ground.

> The men traveling with Saul stood there speechless; they heard the sound but did not see anyone. Saul got up from the ground, but when he opened his eyes he could see nothing. So they led him by the hand into Damascus. For three days he was blind, and did not eat or drink anything. (Acts 9:7-9)

Saul's encounter with Jesus shed light on the sin in his life, and from that day forward, Saul would never be the same. He committed his life to serving and obeying God, bringing the Light to the Gentiles.

Mary. When Mary encountered Jesus outside his tomb, she did not recognize him at first. But when she realized whom she was facing, she fell to her knees in worship. In the book of Acts, we see Mary become a leading woman who accompanied the disciples in their ministry to reach the world with the news of the resurrected Christ. Just like others who have encountered God's holiness, the purpose of her life became clear: she was inspired to obey and immediately wanted others to experience God.

His Holiness Changes Me

Clarity is the ability to see life through God's eyes and not our own. Beth Moore, a leading Bible teacher, captures the clarifying nature of holiness when she writes, "We see Him more clearly and we see ourselves more clearly."[8] When you see God clearly, you will be inspired to obey, and you will want others to experience his glory. God's holiness propels us to act on behalf of those who are mistreated and unloved. Dr. Hunter explains, "God is not a crotchety, self-righteous prude who delights in never doing anything wrong. He is a living, dynamic Being actively involved in making wrong right. He is scintillating light. Holiness is a positive concept and means a life engaged in helping people who hurt."[9]

When you see God clearly, you will be inspired to obey, and you will want others to experience his glory.

Each day millions of children on this planet go hungry and die of neglect. Women are raped, beaten and sold. Murders happen in the name of ethnic cleansing, greed or personal gain. There are deadbeat dads, abortions, crimes and an insurgence of evil that goes largely unnoticed.

While the waves of injustice beat steadily against the shores of our world, we safely lock ourselves away in insulated beach houses of the heart. We know pain exists, because we see it on the television screen and hear it on the radio—but we don't allow the messages of despair to penetrate our well-protected hearts. Work and family become all-consuming, and the trip down the grocery aisle might be the closest we get to rubbing shoulders with those of a different socio-economic level. On occasion we might don the symbol of a cause on our business jacket, but soon it will be replaced by the newest lapel pin and our "lucky" presentation scarf. We might write a check for a good cause now and again, but often it is to please a colleague or make points with a boss.

There is no success without sacrifice. JAN VAN OOSTEN

When I was in college, a group of us were talking idealistically about what we proposed to do to correct the ills of society. My brother-in-law, Jim, said, "The difference between conviction and convenient beliefs are those which you will actually live out over time." I have never forgotten that simple line. I often pray in the crux of a decision, *Lord, give me the backbone to live out the convictions you have called me to. Give me the courage to place your call above my comfort.*

The clarity I pray for can be costly, and it is almost always inconvenient. At a women's retreat in California, Pastor Jan van Oosten of New Covenant Community Church was quoted as saying, "There is no success without sacrifice." God has given the supreme sacrifice for you and me on the cross. What am I willing to sacrifice? What price am I willing to pay? Has my longing for comfort replaced the convictions of my heart?

I know I cannot single-handedly change the entire world, but my prayer is that my heart will be soft enough to respond to God's call when

I encounter his holiness. I pray that you, too, will gain the clarity to see life from heaven's perspective and be inspired to obey.

Winning Words

For the LORD loves the just and will not forsake his faithful ones. They will be protected forever. The King is mighty, he loves justice. Do not follow the crowd in doing wrong. When you give testimony in a lawsuit, do not pervert justice by siding with the crowd. Do not deny justice to your poor people. Do not pervert justice; do not show partiality to the poor or favoritism to the great, but judge your neighbor fairly. Do not pervert justice or show partiality. Do not accept a bribe, for a bribe blinds the eyes of the wise and twists the words of the righteous. Follow justice and justice alone, so that you may live and possess the land the LORD your God is giving you. He will make your righteousness shine like the dawn, the justice of your cause like the noonday sun. Blessed are they who maintain justice, who constantly do what is right.

Good will come to him who is generous and lends freely, who conducts his affairs with justice. When justice is done, it brings joy to the righteous but terror to evildoers. Evil men do not understand justice, but those who seek the LORD understand it fully. The righteous care about justice for the poor, but the wicked have no such concern.

Learn to do right! Seek justice, encourage the oppressed. Defend the cause of the fatherless, plead the case of the widow. Let him who boasts boast about this: that he understands and knows me, that I am the LORD, who exercises kindness, justice and righteousness on earth, for in these I delight. You must return to your God; maintain love and justice, and wait for your God always. Let justice roll on like a river, righteousness like a never-failing stream! [10]

Winning Ways

With so many demands on our time, it's difficult to maintain clarity. In your journal, make a list of ten injustices that you know about in society today and begin praying about what God would have you do to reflect his holy and just character in at least one of those areas.

What keeps you insulated from the pains and ills of society? What can you do to build a bridge to keep in tune to the plight of injustice? Volunteer with a people-helping organization? Make a friend of a different social/economic level? Tutor? Mentor? If you already have such a relationship, do something that expresses how you value that relationship.

Ask God to reveal to you any time you might act unjustly or in an unholy way. Then simply acknowledge these areas when God brings them up. Ask him to show you a better way to respond that more closely reflects his character.

7

$\mathscr{P}$OTENTIAL

"If the first woman God ever made was strong enough
to turn the world upside down all alone,
these women together ought to be able to turn it back
and get it right-side up again."
SOJOURNER TRUTH

$\mathscr{S}$ome moments are frozen in time. In 1851, Frances Gage, an abolitionist and president of the Women's Rights Convention, captured one of those moments in her report on the proceedings of a convention held in Akron, Ohio:

> Sojourner walked to the podium and slowly took off her sunbonnet. Her six-foot frame towered over the audience. She began to speak in her deep, resonant voice: "Well, children, where there is so much racket, there must be something out of kilter, I think between the Negroes of the South and the women of the North—all talking about rights—the white men will be in a fix pretty soon. But what's all this talking about?"
>
> Sojourner pointed to one of the ministers. "That man over there says that women need to be helped into carriages, and lifted over ditches, and to have the best place everywhere. Nobody helps me any best place. And ain't I a woman?"
>
> Sojourner raised herself to her full height. "Look at me! Look at my arm." She bared her right arm and flexed her powerful muscles. "I have plowed, I have planted and I have gathered into barns. And no man could

head me. And ain't I a woman?

"I could work as much, and eat as much as a man—when I could get it—and bear the lash as well! And ain't I a woman? I have borne children and seen most of them sold into slavery, and when I cried out with a mother's grief, none but Jesus heard me. And ain't I a woman?"

The women in the audience began to cheer wildly.

She pointed to another minister. "He talks about this thing in the head. What's that they call it?"

"Intellect," whispered a woman nearby.

"That's it, honey. What's intellect got to do with women's rights or black folks' rights? If my cup won't hold but a pint and yours holds a quart, wouldn't you be mean not to let me have my little half-measure full?

"That little man in black there! He says women can't have as much rights as men. 'Cause Christ wasn't a woman." She stood with outstretched arms and eyes of fire. "Where did your Christ come from?

"Where did your Christ come from?" she thundered again. "From God and a woman! Man had nothing to do with him!" The entire church now roared with deafening applause.

"If the first woman God ever made was strong enough to turn the world upside down all alone, these women together ought to be able to turn it back and get it right-side up again."[1]

The crowd was captivated by her words, as were most people. Historian Mary Arnold notes, "She was a dramatic and inspirational speaker leaving audiences filled with emotion. The simplicity of her language and the sincerity of her message, combined with the courage of her convictions, made Sojourner a sought-after speaker."

Sojourner's amazing confidence was uncharacteristic for both a woman and a Negro during her time in history. Harriet Beecher Stowe once interviewed Sojourner and afterward described her as "self-possessed and at ease. . . . [She had] almost an unconscious superiority, not unmixed with a solemn twinkle of humor. . . . I do not recollect ever to have been conversant with anyone who had more of that silent and subtle power which we call personal presence than this woman."[2]

Out of the Shackles

Sojourner Truth was born Isabella (Belle) Baumfree, the child of slaves.

Sold numerous times, she grew to womanhood as a slave, often doing the work of at least two people. Her duties included acting as a field hand, milkmaid, cleaning woman, weaver, cook and wet nurse. Her owner Dumont bragged that she could do a good family's washing in the night and be ready to go into the field the next morning, where she would do as much raking and binding as his best hands.

Sojourner became a very strong woman, both mentally and physically, during her years of bondage. Through her beatings, she learned determination. As was true of many slaves, Sojourner lost her parents, and was forbidden to see the man she loved. She dealt with her pain privately, and as she was taught in her early childhood, she put away the hurt when it was time to work. Dumont made her marry a slave named Thomas. Together they had five children, and her cruel owner sold most of her children. Sojourner had heard about God from her mother, and she prayed to him every day for relief from her bondage.

Two years before Dumont was legally obligated to set Sojourner free, he approached her with a proposition. He promised her that if she worked extra hard for him over the following year, he would set her free one year early. Wanting freedom and wanting to believe in the integrity of her owner, Sojourner agreed. She put in endless hours of grueling work, but Dumont broke his promise.

Sojourner cried out to God, begging him to help her escape, and the Lord spoke to her:

[He] said to me, "Git up two or three hours afore daylight, an' start off."

So up I got about three o'clock in the mornin', an' I started an' travelled pretty fast, till, when the sun rose, I was clear away from our place an' our folks, an' out o' sight. An' then I begun to think I didn't know nothin' where to go. So I kneeled down, and says I, "Well, Lord, you've started me out, an' now please to show me where to go."

Then the Lord made a house appear to me, an' He said to me that I was to walk on till I saw that house, an' then go in an' ask the people to take me. An' I travelled all day, an' didn't come to the house till late at night; but when I saw it, sure enough, I went in, an' I told the folks that the Lord sent me; an' they was Quakers, an' real kind they was to me. They jes' took me in, an' did for me as kind as ef I'd been one of 'em; an' after they'd give me supper, they took me into a room where here was a great, tall, white bed; an' they told me to sleep there. Well, honey I was kind of skeered when they left me alone with that great white bed ; 'cause I never had been in a bed in my life. It never came into my mind they mean me to sleep in it. An' so I jes' camped down under it, on the floor, an' then I slep' pretty well. In the mornin', when they came in, they asked me if I hadn't been asleep; an' I said "Yes, I never slep' better."[3]

Sojourner lived with the Quaker family for a few years, and with their help, she won a lawsuit to have her son Peter returned to her—freed from slavery. But while she was there, she stopped praying, thinking that she didn't need God anymore. It wasn't until she won her own freedom in 1828 under the New York State Anti-slavery Act, that she encountered God again.

An' says I, "O God, I didn't know as you was so great! An' I turned right around an' come into the house, an' set down in my room; for 't was God all around me. I could feel it burnin', burnin', burnin' all around me, an' goin' through me! I saw I was so wicked, it seemed as if it would burn me up. Ah I said, "O somebody, somebody, stand between God an' me for it burns me." Then, honey, I said so, I felt as it were somethin' like an ambrill [umbrella]—somebody that stood between me an' the light, an' I felt it was SOMEBODY—somebody that stood between me an' God; an' it felt cool, like shade; an' says I, "Who's this that stands between me an' God? . . "Who is this?" . . . . I began to feel 't was somebody that loved me; an' I tried to know him. . . . An' finally somethin' spoke out in me an' said, THIS IS JESUS! An' I spoke out with all my might, an' says I, "THIS IS JESUS! Glory be to God!" An' then the whole world grew bright, an' I said "Praise, praise, praise the Lord!" An' I begun to feel such a love in my soul as I never felt before— love to all creatures. An' then, all of the sudden it stopped, an' I said, "Dar's the white folks, that have abused an' beat you an' abused your people." But then there came another rush of love through my soul, an' I cried out loud, "Lord, Lord, I can love even the white folks."

Honey, I jes' walked round an' round in a dream. Jesus loved me! I knowed it—I felt it. Jesus was my Jesus. Jesus would love me always.[4]

Soon afterward, Sojourner changed her name to reflect the change of heart she'd had.

My name was Isabella; but when I left the house of bondage, I left everything behind. I w'n't goin' to keep nothin' of Egypt on me, an' so I went to the Lord an' asked him to give me a new name. And the Lord gave me Sojourner, because I was to travel up an' down the land, showin' the people their sins, an' bein' a sign unto them. Afterwards I told the Lord I wanted another name, 'cause everybody else had two names; and the Lord gave me Truth, because I was to declare the truth to the people.[5]

Sojourner Truth went on to become an active spokesperson for the gospel, traveling, setting up a banner, gathering a crowd and preaching to them night after night. She became a famous preacher, speaking out for women's rights and abolition, but mostly she preached a living gospel that drew people to a personal relationship with Jesus Christ. Sojourner didn't let her illiteracy, her gender or her former slave status hold her back from speaking out; she knew her potential came from being a redeemed woman with a passion to spread the same message of hope, help and redemption that she had experienced.

Free to Reach God's Potential

We all have chains of lies and half-truths that shackle us, robbing us of achievement, blocking us from arriving at our full potential. I was no different; as a child I was burdened by my father's demands for perfection. In junior high, I brought home a report card that read: 100%, 100%, 100%, 100%, 100%, 99.9%. My father, who had been drinking, demanded, "Pam, why isn't that a 100?"

I felt paralyzed by his demands for perfection. For years I thought that if I only had perfect grades, then I'd feel loved. Or if I only dated the coolest guy with the coolest car, then I could achieve in life. Or maybe if I gained recognition for being a cheerleader, homecoming queen, scholarship winner, then I'd feel validated and could succeed. But even when I pushed myself to achieve those things, I felt empty inside.

It wasn't until God took me to a verse that said, "We cry out to him, Abba, Father" that I realized the God who created everything and everyone, the God who held all power and all knowledge, was reaching out and wanted to know me—not push me, not berate me—but know me, like a friend. That was the day I began to reach my potential. I was free to achieve because my achievement didn't depend solely on what I could do, but on what God had already done for me. I knew that God loved me. I was no longer shackled by perfectionism, but freed to soar, to be lifted by God into my potential.

God sees your potential long before you do, and he longs to answer the heart of those who seek him.

You can also experience the chains and shackles being removed in your own life by crying out to God. James 4:8 says, "Come near to God and he will come near to you." When God hears the seeker's heart, he reaches out. "For the eyes of the LORD range throughout the earth to strengthen those whose hearts are fully committed to him" (2 Chron 16:9). He sees your potential long before you do, and he longs to answer the heart of those who seek him:

> But if from there you seek the LORD your God, you will find him if you look for him with all your heart and with all your soul. (Deut 4:29)

> For the LORD searches every heart and understands every motive behind the thoughts. If you seek him, he will be found by you; but if you forsake him, he will reject you forever. (1 Chron 28:9)

> I love those who love me, and those who seek me find me. (Prov 8:17)

> The Lord is not slow in keeping his promise, as some understand slowness. He is patient with you, not wanting anyone to perish, but everyone to come to repentance. (2 Pet 3:9)

When God reaches out to us, we are changed. He gives us confidence—a confidence so beyond our own power that it seems unlikely, uncanny, unprecedented. It's a confidence and power beyond our own measurable skills, talent and intellect. It's a promise God makes when he impassions our hearts: "Not that we are competent in ourselves to claim anything for ourselves, but our competence comes from God" (2 Cor 3:5).

A Response to Love

The natural response to coming into a personal relationship with God is an overwhelming passion to extend that same opportunity to others. But sometimes those of us with talent, skill and credentials are frustrated because the passion comes with his power—*not our own*. But there's a good reason for God's logic in this:

> Brothers, think of what you were when you were called. Not many of you were wise by human standards; not many were influential; not many were of noble birth. But God chose the foolish things of the world to shame the wise; God chose the weak things of the world to shame the strong. He chose the lowly things of this world and the despised things—and the things that are not—to nullify the things that are, so that no one may boast before him. It is because of him that you are in Christ Jesus, who has become for us wisdom from God—that is, our righteousness, holiness and redemption. Therefore, as it is written: "Let him who boasts boast in the Lord." (1 Cor 1:26-31)

It seems that God is most pleased when we entrust our gifts and talents to him, to his timing, for his use. "Humble yourselves, therefore, under God's mighty hand, that he may lift you up in due time" (1 Pet 5:6).

To humble means "to depress."[6] Humbling ourselves is a voluntary action, placing ourselves under God's hand, like a child nestling under the loving arm of a parent. From this place of shelter, the child waits, is nurtured, and at just the right time, the parent's loving arm pushes the child to center stage.

As we bow low in worship, God gives us the ability to rise and soar into our potential. We are empowered by his love.

Micah 6:8 makes clear that humility is a concept vital to our success: "He has showed you, O man, what is good. And what does the Lord require of you? To act justly and to love mercy and to walk humbly with your God." In Hebrew, the word *humbly* implies a stance of bowing, stooping or crouching as in worship.[7] Worship is the act of acknowledging God for who he is. It is no wonder that in knowing who God is, we gain the confidence to live our lives with the potential that God has given us: "The people that do know their God shall be strong" (Dan 11:32 KJV). As we bow low in worship, God gives us the ability to rise and soar into our potential. We are empowered by his love.

Winning Words

I saw the Lord seated on a throne, high and exalted, and the train of his robe filled the temple. Above him were seraphs, each with six wings: With two wings they covered their faces, with two they covered their feet, and with two they were flying. And they were calling to one another:

"Holy, holy, holy is the Lord Almighty;
the whole earth is full of his glory."

At the sound of their voices the doorposts and thresholds shook and the temple was filled with smoke.

"Woe to me!" I cried. "I am ruined! For I am a man of unclean lips, and I live among a people of unclean lips, and my eyes have seen the King, the LORD Almighty."

Then one of the seraphs flew to me with a live coal in his hand, which he had taken with tongs from the altar. With it he touched my mouth and said, "See, this has touched your lips; your guilt is taken away and your sin atoned for."

Then I heard the voice of the Lord saying, "Whom shall I send? And who will go for us?"

And I said, "Here am I. Send me!"[8]

Winning Ways

Have you humbled yourself and sought after God's will for your life? Try these exercises for practicing humility in your life:

☐ Go one day without pointing out to others your contributions or credits.

☐ All week compliment and encourage anyone who makes you look good or helps you succeed in your goals.

☐ When given a compliment, practice silently thanking God for equipping and enabling your success.

☐ Ask God to show you your potential by choosing to see yourself as he sees you. He loved you enough to die for you. In your journal, begin to record any verses that help you see yourself the same as how God sees you. Also make a list of ways that you can see God's love for you.

8

*N*ETWORKING

"I don't network; I make friends."
LINDA RILEY

*T*he streets were covered with ice, and the radio was recommending people stay off the roads. But Mary Kay had scheduled a home demonstration of Stanley Home Products, and she had promised to show up, come rain, shine, sleet or snow. When she arrived, she soon discovered only one other person besides the hostess would be at the party. This guest was the hostess's child's Sunday school teacher, and she too felt an obligation to be at the party.

Mary Kay decided the personal touch was in order, so she set the formal presentation aside and simply chatted with the two women over coffee and cake. Mary Kay noticed that the guest, Mary Crowley, had a real charismatic personality, and as the evening progressed they began to compare notes on their lives. Like Mary Kay, Mary had young children at home, and when Mary Kay explained how she navigated her day to skirt the Dallas area traffic so she could be home by four o'clock each afternoon, Mary seemed impressed and curious.

Mary worked as the assistant to the president of a purse manufacturing company. She told Mary Kay how much she earned and then asked Mary Kay what she was making in sales, to which Mary Kay replied she made the same—in a very bad week of sales. Mary Kay offered her new friend a job in sales at her company, but Mary didn't take her up on her offer.

About a month later, however, Mary called Mary Kay. Her husband was going to be stationed out of town for several months with the National Guard, and Mary wanted to try sales part-time.

Within a few months she became a full-time dealer—and she was terrific. Because Mary was in Mary Kay's unit, the entire unit soared. And when Mary Kay was transferred to St. Louis with her husband's job, the company allowed Mary to take over Mary Kay's territory, and she consistently earned tremendous commissions until she left to take a position as sales manager for a new company, World Gifts.

A year later, when Mary Kay returned to Texas, she stopped to visit her friend Mary. This time Mary recruited Mary Kay to a position at World Gifts! Within a year, Mary Kay's unit was doing a major portion of the company's total business sales.

New Look at Networking

Networking is typically seen as the making and using of relationships for your own personal gain, a kind of "I'll scratch your back, you scratch mine" mentality, but the Christian is challenged to a higher standard of "If you want to be great in God's kingdom, be the servant of all" and "Seek ye first the kingdom of God, then all these things shall be added unto you."

Good networkers have an open hand with their opportunities, seeing that the best in life is a gift from God and they are just a funnel for opportunity and good fortune.

Mary Kay and Mary understood that those who are strong networkers are so because they sincerely value people. Often it is their love of people that God uses to create opportunity. Good networkers have an open hand with their opportunities, seeing that the best in life is a gift from God and they are just a funnel for opportunity and good fortune. Good networkers see that sharing opportunity, rather than selfishly hiding or holding opportunity, means that God multiplies the very opportunity they are sharing with others.

While at World Gifts, Mary tried to instill these ideas in her sales team of five hundred women: "I taught the staff to think of the customers and hostesses as people with needs first, and customers second. We had rallies, seminars, and a lot of good fellowship." But her life was about to turn upside-down.

> I took a group of top producers to Mexico City, and I discovered that the owner had scheduled a cocktail party as one of the activities. I didn't like that one bit and I told him so. (I was very firm in my belief that alcoholic beverages did not fit in with my purpose of building people.)
>
> He replied, "You can't run the sales department as though it's a Baptist Sunday School, Mary."[1]

After this exchange, the owner of the company let Mary know that he was no longer going to bend to her wishes. And then, just when her sales team was beginning to make good incomes from outstanding sales, he put limits on commissions. Going to bat for her team, Mary wrote a letter to her boss outlining her concerns. Mary explains:

> I felt really badly about the differences and hoped he would see things my way. But by the following Monday at 7 a.m., I heard the sound of a truck in my driveway, and then the ringing of my doorbell. It was the man from the company warehouse. "Here's your furniture," he said. "The boss told me you wouldn't be using it anymore."
>
> They stood there, empty and meaningless as an abandoned house, a reminder of the beginning four and a half years ago—when both my furniture and philosophies were welcome and wanted. Now, neither were wanted anymore. I threw myself down on the sofa and started to cry.

Mary felt unwanted and unmotivated, but it seemed God was saying, "Don't just sit there and feel sorry for yourself." Mary had taught her team to set their goals high: "Fail if you have to. Daring generates excitement, excitement generates enthusiasm, enthusiasm generates energy." Now God was holding her to it.

Mary dried her tears, showered, put on her nicest suit and called on some of her connections. First she went to see a friend who was successful in sales as well. Immediately he offered her a job. But she didn't take it. What she really wanted to do was start her own company, one where she could set the standards, but she wasn't sure where to start:

> If I had my own company, I could set the standards I wanted upheld. I
> could be as generous as I wanted with commissions. What would happen if
> I started a business that was really dedicated to helping women create hap-
> pier homes? Wouldn't it just have to succeed?
>
> But how could I create such a company? Nobody knew me, and I
> didn't have the capital or contacts with suppliers. Or so I thought.

On impulse, Mary went to a large importer of decorative accessories —
an importer that had supplied her ex-staff with merchandise. When she
walked in, she was recognized immediately and given a credit line for
their products.

It seemed God was paving the path before her. But she wanted her
husband's blessing—and when he had left her that morning she was in
tears on the sofa. That evening he found her bubbling over with excitement. Her husband's reply was, "Honey, if you don't go into business, the
world of business will be the loser."

Mary's company, Home Interiors and Gifts, was a huge success. Mary
found herself invited to the White House, giving away Christmas shopping
sprees, supporting many charitable causes, funding the start-up of a company owned and operated by the disabled, and funding an entire new
building for children at her church. At the dedication service, her son Don
told the congregation, "When I was a little boy riding the bus to church
here on Sundays, I used to see my mother working two jobs just to put
food on the table. She was so hardheaded, she said we were going to tithe.
And at that time I thought, 'We could sure use that money for other
things.' Now I see how God has taken that money and blessed through it."

People Are the Product

Like Mary, Mary Kay wanted to create opportunities for others. After
spending twenty-five years as a professional sales woman, Mary Kay
retired and decided to create her own company, now called Mary Kay
Cosmetics.

Why would a retired woman start a company? For most of her life,
Mary Kay was a single parent trying to provide for her family, and she

had been frustrated by the lack of opportunity for women.

> One company paid me $25,000 a year to be a National Training Director, but in truth, I was acting as the National Sales Manager—and for a salary much less than the job was worth. Then there were the times when I would be asked to take a man out on the road to train him, and after six months of training, he would be brought back to Dallas, made my superior, and given twice the salary! It happened more than once. What really angered me was when I was told that these men earned more because they had families to support. I had a family to support, too.[2]

With Mary Kay Cosmetics, Mary Kay offered a chance for women to achieve their dreams and goals. "My objective was to give women the opportunity to do anything they were smart enough to do. And so to me, 'P and L' meant more than profit and loss; it meant people and love."

Mary Kay founded her company on her down-home Southern values rooted in biblical truths. "When you put God first, family second, and your career third, everything seems to work out." Mary Kay goes on to explain, "When you get to the bottom line, it doesn't matter how much money you've made, how big your house is, or how many cars you own. For on that day when God calls you to accept your relationship with Jesus Christ, nothing else matters."

Mary Kay wanted to be at the helm of a company that was run by the golden rule, "Do to others as you would have them do to you" (Lk 6:31).

> At Mary Kay Cosmetics, we focus on giving, not just getting, and we use this philosophy in every aspect of the company. For example, we use the Go-Give principle when teaching our Beauty Consultants the art of customer relations. We constantly stress that a consultant must never have dollar signs in her eyes or think, "How much can I sell today?" Instead, she must think in terms of "What can I do today so that these women will leave here feeling better about themselves? How can I help each woman develop a more positive self-image?"

Mary Kay is adamant about encouraging her employees to encourage and praise each other. Being positive and enthusiastic is a company mantra. Mary Kay notes, "The enthusiasm comes from a Greek word meaning 'God within.'"

One of Mary Kay's favorite stories of instilling confidence is the story of a new consultant, Ruby Lee, who was so shy she couldn't even say "good morning" and look the person in the face. Ruby Lee's unit encouraged and praised her, though, and one year from her training date, Ruby Lee was delivering a speech to thousands at the yearly seminar. The audience was spell bound, and she received a standing ovation. Now she is a National Sales Director in the company.

"It's a really good day to me if just one more woman discovers how great she really is and how much potential she has," notes Mary Kay.

> One of the most important steps I ever took was when I began imagining that every single person I met had a sign around his or her neck that read, "Make me feel important." Whether it's figuratively or literal—absolutely everyone responds to applause. I believe that if you had the choice of two gifts for your child—$1 million on one side of the scale and the ability to think positively on the other—the greater gift would be the gift of confidence. And you only give confidence with praise and applause.

"It was . . . my theory that if you build the people, the people will build the business. If you help other people get what they want out of life, then you will get what you want out of life."

Mary Kay's principles and values paid off. In 1984 Mary Kay Cosmetics was named one of the one hundred best companies to work for in America and was the only one in fifty-five to repeat that distinction when the second edition was printed in 1993. The company was also listed as one of the ten best companies for women to work for.

Giving Back
Good networkers are grateful and seek to give back to the people and places that helped them gain. Mary Kay was asked by her pastor to give an inspirational announcement to help raise funds for a new children's educational building at the church she was attending. At the rate the church was going—only $600-$1,000 was being donated per week by the congregation—the building wouldn't be finished until these children were grownups with children of their own. She agreed to give an inspirational challenge six weeks out, but due to a hectic schedule, she waited

until the last minute to prepare the exact words. She had a habit of getting up at five o'clock every morning, but this particular Sunday, the alarm didn't go off, and she found herself frantically praying for God's guidance on what to say: *Lord, fill my mouth with worthwhile words, and stop me when I've said enough.* As she prayed she felt God impress upon her what she was to say, "Mary Kay, tell the congregation that today you will match whatever they give today."

Good networkers are grateful and seek to give back to the people and places that helped them gain.

As she walked to the podium she realized she still didn't know exactly what she was going to say. *This is in your hands, Lord.* Mary Kay explained how she felt that it was important that children learn about God while they are young and quoted Proverbs 22:6, "Train up a child in the way he should go, and when he is old he will not depart from it." Then she said,

> You know, we've been talking about this building for quite some time. And each Sunday we've been getting about $600. On a good week, we might even get $1,000. But at this rate, these children are going to have grandchildren before the building is built. We must do something about this. You've heard me talk about our company and how we operate on a cash basis. Well, I'll match whatever you give today. . . . I don't want pledges from you today—I want cash or checks! Whatever you give today, I'll match.

Then Mary Kay waited for the call. She was hoping the congregation had given at least a little more than they normally did—$2,000, $5,000, or maybe even $10,000. When she finally got a call the next morning, the deacon started explaining that the church board had a special meeting the night before and that they had decided that they wouldn't hold Mary Kay to her end of the bargain.

"I made the offer, I will stick to it," said Mary Kay. She began to get excited that maybe her hopes of raising a bit more for the church had been accomplished. She asked how much had been donated by the congregation.

His reply was astonishing. $107,748! Instantly, Mary Kay was elated, and then the reality of the amount hit her. Although the company and she as an individual could obviously afford to match the funds, she knew she didn't have that much cash readily accessible, so she shot up another prayer to God for help. *Okay, Lord, You got me into this. Now get me out! How am I going to get this money?*

Just then the phone rang, and it was her son Richard. "Everything I put in your hands turns to gold! Those oil wells . . . they've just come in. . . . It's unbelievable. Do you know what those wells are worth? . . . Between the two of them, your share this month will be more than $100,000."

Mary Kay adds, "I've said it before, but now I'll say it even stronger—you can't outgive God!"

Network with God First

The source for Mary Kay's and Mary's enthusiasm and positive attitudes can be traced back to their most important relationship—their relationship with God. Mary Kay explains, "I believe we have found success because God has led us all the way. Often it's the little, daily decisions—the ones you make hour by hour—that mean the difference between success and failure. And I feel that God put His protective arm around us and guided us to the right path."

In networking, God brings people together and uses their lives to spread the opportunity to experience his love and joy.

Both Mary Kay and Mary have been honored with the Horatio Alger Award, an award that recognizes the success and achievements of Americans who are committed to sharing a message of hope and encouragement. In receiving their awards both Mary Kay and Mary reinforced the importance of knowing God and seeing people as God sees them. In her acceptance speech, Mary enthusiastically commented, "I think one person with belief is equal to a force of 99 with only an interest. And I have belief. I believe in the Creator who made me in His image. Because of that fact, I am 'somebody.' Consequently,

I am able to look at everybody else as a 'somebody' too."

And when Mary Kay was asked by *60 Minutes* host Morley Safer, "Now I have been around here a couple of days, and every time I turn around I hear the word God. Aren't you really just using God?" Mary Kay looked him squarely in the eyes and gently replied, "No, Mr. Safer, I sincerely hope it's the other way around—that God is using me."

In networking, God brings people together and uses their lives to spread the opportunity to experience his love and joy. He took Mary Kay's ordinary faithful commitment as a salesperson for Stanley Home Products and turned it into extraordinary connection. What routine commitment in your life will he use to transform you?

Winning Words

Turn, O Lord, and deliver me; save me because of your unfailing love. Show the wonder of your great love, you who save by your right hand those who take refuge in you from their foes. I love you, O LORD, my strength. For the king trusts in the LORD; through the unfailing love of the Most High he will not be shaken. . . . For your love is ever before me, and I walk continually in your truth. Let your face shine on your servant; save me in your unfailing love. Many are the woes of the wicked, but the LORD's unfailing love surrounds the man who trusts in him. But the eyes of the LORD are on those who fear him, on those whose hope is in his unfailing love, May your unfailing love rest upon us, O LORD, even as we put our hope in you. Continue your love to those who know you, your righteousness to the upright in heart. Rise up and help us; redeem us because of your unfailing love. For great is your love, reaching to the heavens; your faithfulness reaches to the skies. But I will sing of your strength, in the morning I will sing of your love; for you are my fortress, my refuge in times of trouble. When I said, "My foot is slipping," your love, O LORD, supported me. May your unfailing love be my comfort, according to your promise to your servant. Let the morning bring me word of your unfailing love, for I have put my trust in you. Show me the way I should go, for to you I lift up my soul. . . . the LORD delights in those who fear him, who put their hope in his unfailing love.[3]

Winning Ways

"I don't network, I make friends" implies that networking can sometimes be self-serving. I use my friend Linda Riley's philosophy as a motive check on how I treat people who could possibly have a positive impact on my life if they were a part of my world. Because of my friendship with Linda, I now see networking as an opportunity to serve others. It is my goal to help others succeed, and I trust that God will bless that servant's attitude and give me what I need to succeed. God has called me to make connections to himself, to opportunities and to others. How about you? How do you handle your friendships? The book of Proverbs says "Iron sharpens iron, so one man sharpens another" (27:17). Use the questions below to do a friendship check on how you treat others:

☐ Do I seek to bring out the best in others, even if it means they will outshine me?

☐ Do I do unto others as I would have done unto me?

☐ Do I keep confidences?

☐ Do I promote unity and win-win outcomes?

☐ Do I try to reciprocate when loyalty, favors and appreciation are given to me?

☐ Do I desire to create opportunities rather than obstacles for others?

Sometimes writing up a personal motto or a creed of purpose or integrity helps keep us on track when it comes to serving others. My personal mission is to encourage and equip women to be all God designed them to be. Mary Crowley had many short statements that served a guideposts to her life and business. Mary chose some life essentials:

☐ Learning to develop your character in God's image,

☐ Faithfulness in your family life,

☐ Absolute honesty on the job,

☐ Helping those who need you.[4]

Mary also decided she would use the Rotary Club four-way test as part of her business philosophy:

☐ Is it the truth?

☐ Is it fair to all concerned?

☐ Will it build good and better friendships?

☐ Will it be beneficial to all concerned?[5]

Influenced by Josh McDowell, I encourage women to ask three simple questions: Does this show love for God? for others? for myself?

Have you written a personal motto or defined the principles that will guide your actions? If not, take the time to write a mission statement, a purpose statement, something that captures your heart and passion. Then frame it, have it engraved on something for your desk or office, or place it on your business card holder in your briefcase or purse. Then choose a life verse, one Bible verse that you'd like to use as an integrity reminder when you are tempted to cut corners in regard to the way you treat people. Commit this verse to memory or write it out and place it next to your mission statement so that you will have a daily visual reminder of who you are before God.

9

$\mathcal{P}$EACE

---

*"A woman is like a teabag:
Only in hot water do you realize how strong she is."*
NANCY REAGAN

$\mathcal{I}$ had been out running errands. As I walked into the house, the phone was ringing. It was the phone call that no mother ever wants to receive.

"Pam—" said my husband, Bill. He sounded scared, and he struggled with the words he was weighing out. "The sheriff wants you to bring as many photos of Caleb as you can find. Pam, the boys are missing."

I hung up the phone and burst into tears. My Caleb was only five years old. How could he be missing? He had been at his best friend's house playing, and now he and his friend were gone.

I looked around for photos of Caleb, but I couldn't see any. My eyes blurred with tears of panic. *God, Caleb needs me right now. I need to find pictures. Please be with my Caleb, and help me be the kind of mom Caleb needs. Give me your peace.*

A supernatural calm entered my soul, and as I looked up I could see that there were photos of Caleb all over the wall and albums of them on the shelf. I grabbed them and ran out the door.

As I headed across town, I panicked again. *What was he wearing? What did I put on him this morning?* I couldn't remember. *I must be a terrible*

mother! I can't even remember what I put on my little boy! God, I need your peace!
I can't think. God, please help me be the kind of mom Caleb needs. Help me remem-
ber. Give me peace so I can think. Protect Caleb and give him peace.

Then I remembered: Caleb was wearing a striped shirt, black sweat-
pants, brown boots—and that wonderful curly blond hair. Tears puddled
in my eyes and flowed down my cheeks. I blinked and frantically wiped
my eyes so I could see the road. *God, give me your peace. Help me make it to*
Gail's safely.

I thought of my friend Gail, and I empathized with how frantic she
must be feeling as well. What would I say to her? I knew she was a great
mom, attentive and caring. *She's as freaked out as me right now,* I thought. *God,*
what am I going to say to Gail? Give Gail peace. Help me be the kind of friend I need
to be right now. Be with our two little boys. Give them your peace and protection.

As I turned the corner, I saw Gail in the center of her yard. I ran from
my car, wrapped my arms around her and said, "Gail, I love you. We will
get through this together." We begged God to watch over the boys and to
give us peace so we could be strong. Patrol cars were speeding to the
scene, and my husband appeared from behind the house.

"Not there, either," he said.

Then he saw me. He wrapped his arms around me, and he prayed,
"God, help us find our precious Caleb."

The sheriff interrupted. "We are sending out all available squad cars,
and they have dispatched two helicopters. Are those the pictures of your
children?" He asked a few more questions, then said, "We would like one
parent of each child to stay here with me at the command post." Bill suggested the Gail and I stay, and he volunteered to lead the charge into the
countryside of overgrown brush filled with transients, wild animals and
even criminals.

I called my friend Penny and had her call neighborhood watch, the
school, the people in our church and her mom's friends in the adjoining
retirement community. My older two sons, Brock and Zach, went
together through the neighborhood and caught kids coming off school
buses to tell them to keep an eye out. Worried parents appeared from
their homes to help in the search. Soon hundreds of volunteers were out
looking for two lost five-year-old boys.

When Brock and Zach returned, I sent them home with one of my best friends in case Caleb had tried walking home, five miles away. As they pulled away, I saw their worried faces peering back at me, and the panic and fear began to rise again. *Lord, please give Brock and Zach peace. I can't see them or Bill, and they can't see me. And Caleb can't see any of us! We all need your peace!*

The sheriff in command asked me, "What time is it, Mrs. Farrel?" I looked at my watch—the hours were ticking away! Two hours had already passed. Soon two helicopters appeared overhead, announcing a description of our missing boys. I looked at Gail. Tears were streaming down both our faces. This was real. This was a nightmare.

God, be with Caleb. I know your Word. You say you hem him in before and behind. You say all things are held in the palm of your hand. You say that all the angels are at your command. Send your angels. Put a hedge of protection around those boys. Be with my Caleb. He knows you. Your spirit resides inside him. Give him your peace. Wrap your love around him. And God be with Bill too. Give him your peace. God, help me be the kind of mom I need to be. It won't help anyone if I break down. Give me your peace, your strength, your hope.

A supernatural calm reassured my heart. I began to pray specifically for Caleb, imagining how he must feel. *Lord, let your presence be a shelter to him. You say you shelter us under your wings. Shelter Caleb. You say you are a fortress and a deliverer. Deliver Caleb.*

"Mrs. Farrel, what time is it?" the officer asked. I told him; over three hours had gone by. I began to cry as I sensed the precious time ebbing away. I prayed, *God, you know all things. I take my stand in you and your shed blood on the cross. I command all evil be sent away through your power.* The peace returned, and I continued to pray for Caleb and direct the stream of new volunteers that kept arriving.

"Mrs. Farrel, what time is it?" the officer asked again. I wanted to scream at him, "Get a watch!" But I didn't. I looked at my watch, told the officer the time and continued to pray, *Lord, help me be the kind of citizen I need to be right now.*

"It's been four hours," the officer said, stating what I already knew. "If we don't find the boys in the next few minutes, we will have to go down the street to the fire station and set up a permanent command post."

The words slapped me in the face. I knew what that meant, and it was not good news. I'd seen all the John Walsh films. I'd shown "Stranger Danger." This was bad news. This was the loss of hope. This was the beginning of the end.

God, you say you are in control, and I believe that. I am going to choose right now, that no matter what happens, I will hang on to you. I've seen families go through tragedy. The families that make it have chosen you. I know the statistics that the death of a child means the break-up of over 90 percent of marriages that experience that trauma. I know the only hope and help for my family is to believe you are who you say you are. God, your Word says that you are good and you are wholly good. It says you can turn dark into light and work all things together for good, so right now I am choosing to believe. And even if they bring my precious Caleb to me dead across their arms, I will choose to believe the truth of who you are. It is the only hope. I can choose despair or I can choose you. I choose you. Give us your presence—Caleb, Bill, Brock, Zach and me. God, I am claiming and standing in your peace!

A voice shook me from my daze of prayer. I saw a squad car pull up and two officers talking. The commander approached.

"We have received a sighting of two youths. We don't have any confirmation, but we are sending a squad car by to see if the two children are your sons. Please, we don't have confirmation."

"But we have hope," I said, smiling. The time ticked by. Gail and I continued to pray for God's peace. Bill heard the news and came running back to the house. About twenty minutes later, a squad car pulled up. Two doors popped open, and out tumbled two tousled, dirty boys—our boys! I ran to Caleb. I wrapped my arms around Caleb and said, "I love you, Caleb!"

I heard a quiet but relieved "I love you, Mommy." Bill gave him a hug and exchanged "I love you's," and then we asked, "Where have you been?"

To make a long story short, here's what happened: Caleb went to his friend's house to play after school, and while they were eating fresh-baked cookies on the front patio, Gail stepped inside to check on her last batch of cookies. Gail's five-year-old son asked Caleb, "You want to go on a great adventure?" Caleb quickly agreed; this was a simple game they normally played in the safety of the schoolyard, so off they went around the corner and down the street a few blocks.

When Gail returned the boys were gone. She looked everywhere, and when Bill called to check on Caleb, she told him the news, "I can't find the boys. I've looked everywhere. I've just called the police." When Bill arrived at Gail's a few minutes later, the police were already there, and that's when Bill called me.

Meanwhile, our boys walked past my friend Carol's house. Carol normally would have been stepping out to go pick up her children from school at that time, but she was ill when the boys passed her home. So the boys continued unnoticed and soon stopped to play on some playground equipment at an apartment complex nearby. Later, we heard that one mother drove by and thought the boys looked too young to be left by themselves, but the apartments always seemed to have unattended children, so against her better judgment, she drove on.

Then Caleb's friend saw a mobile home park across the street and said, "My babysitter lives there! Let's go see her." (His babysitter actually lived in a mobile home park in another city, but the boys were too young to know any different.) As they waited at the light at the busiest four-lane road in our community, a mother saw the boys and thought they were very young to be crossing the street by themselves. But her teen daughter scolded her, "Oh, Mom, you're so overprotective." So they too went on.

When the light turned green, the boys sped across the street, played in some people's yards and then went underground into a huge storm tunnel, where they stayed for the hours we were looking for them.

We're not sure whether they got tired, hungry, afraid or had to go to the bathroom, but the boys finally popped their heads out from the storm drain. The manager of the mobile home park, a kindly grandmother, had rallied the retirees of the park, and everyone was out looking for our two boys. When she finally spotted them, she said, "Now boys, I think your parents are very worried about you. Why don't we get into my golf cart and go call the police so you can get back to your parents?"

Caleb piped up, "Oh ma'am, we can't get in your golf cart. You're a stranger." (He can run away for over four hours when he's not even been allowed to go out of the front yard before, but he won't ride with a stranger!) Just then, a parent from our school drove in the park and saw what was happening. He got out of the car with his daughter and said, "Hi guys, you know me, you know my daughter. Why don't we all get in the golf cart and go call the police!"

That was the longest day of my life—but God gave peace. The same peace that I've seen him give to parents at hospital bedsides, and the same peace he gives at the graveside. Supernatural peace that goes beyond comprehension. Peace that brings sanity in insane situations. Peace that is solid when it feels like you've just stepped into the quicksand. I didn't know that day what the outcome would be, but I knew my only hope for that moment, or the moments ahead, was in banking on the character of God, the giver of peace.

For This I Have Jesus

British theologian Charles Price shares a story of a painting contest in England where the theme of the contest was peace. Most of the paintings depicted serene settings; however, the winning painting depicted a raging storm beating mercilessly against a cliff. Tucked into the cleft of a rock on the cliff was one tiny nest; a ray of light broke through the dark storm clouds and encircled the nest, where a gull was peacefully sleeping, safe from the torrential surroundings.

We tend to see peace as the absence of trouble; rather, peace is God's calming presence in the midst of trouble.

We tend to see peace as the absence of trouble; rather, peace is God's calming presence in the midst of trouble. The Bible tells us that one of God's names is Jehovah Shalom, meaning "the Lord is our peace." Time and again the Bible confirms God as the giver of peace. I am so grateful that I had Jesus the day Caleb was missing. It was my relationship with God that pulled me through. It was his very presence that brought us peace.

It has been years since the day Caleb was missing, but every time I leave my family for a speaking engagement, any time one of my boys visits friends, relatives or goes on activities out of my sight, or whenever the storms of life threaten to pull me under, I tuck myself like a bird under the cleft of God's character. I have learned that true strength comes not from having life under our control but from the surety that life is under God's control. Then and only then can we find inner peace.

True strength comes not from having life under our control but from the surety that life is under God's control. Then and only then can we find inner peace.

Charles Price had a mentor in ministry, John Hunter, one of Britain's leading evangelists who became known for preaching hope and peace and for the saying, "For this I have Jesus." One day Charles Price heard that his dear mentor was had suffered two successive strokes, so Charles called to offer his love and prayers. John Hunter's wife prepared Charles for the worst. She explained that her husband had slurred speech and wasn't sure how much he would be able to communicate, but she knew he would be delighted to hear from Charles so she held the phone up to her husband.

For this I have Jesus. JOHN HUNTER

"I am so sorry you are going through this difficulty," Charles said.

Through slurred speech, Pastor Hunter replied, "For this I have Jesus."[1]

For this I have Jesus. That one line of hope has been repeated throughout time in face of tragedy, crisis and stress. When life feels out of your control, remember that it is not out of God's control. The same Jesus who said to the waves, "Be still," can calm the waters of your life, but more important, he can give you peace in the midst of the storm. For this you have Jesus.

Winning Words

The LORD turn his face toward you and give you peace. May there be the LORD's peace forever. The LORD gives strength to his people; the LORD blesses his people with peace. He will stand and shepherd his flock in the strength of the LORD, in the majesty of the name of the LORD his God. And they will live securely, for then his greatness will reach to the ends of the earth. And he will be there peace. Peace I leave with you; my peace I give you. . . . Do not let your hearts be troubled and do not be afraid. I have told you these things, so that in me you may have peace. We have peace with God through our Lord Jesus Christ . . . and we rejoice in the hope of the glory of God. For God is not a God of disorder but of peace. For he himself is our peace. And the peace of God, which transcends all understanding, will guard your hearts and your minds in Christ Jesus. Let the peace of Christ rule in your hearts, since as members of one body you were called to peace. Now may the Lord of peace himself give you peace at all times and in every way.[2]

Winning Ways

How well do you know Jesus? Do you have verses memorized that show his character, that give you a glimpse of his majesty, show his person through the names he was called? In the book of John, Jesus gives many word pictures of who he is. These metaphors can give you peace and strength in the midst of the storms of life.

Jesus is the Word; when you need clarification, wisdom, discernment, then look to the ultimate guide (Jn 1:1).

He is the light; when you need guidance, look to him for your next step (Jn 1:4; 8:12; 9:5).

He is the bread of life; when you feel empty inside, look to him for fulfillment (Jn 6:35, 41, 48, 51).

Jesus is from above; when you need perspective, look to him and ask to see life from his vantage point. (Jn 8:23-24; 12:32).

Jesus is the Son of Man. He is truly human, sympathetic to our frailties, yet he was perfect, so when you are feeling fragile, fallible and frail, look to your sympathetic Lord for aid (Jn 8:28).[3]

Jesus is the gate for the sheep. When you need a place of safety, go to him and you'll find rest (Jn 10:7, 14).

Jesus is God's Son. When you need power beyond your own to cope with life, take your concern to him (Jn 10:36).

Jesus is the resurrection. If your life feels dead, if you feel hopeless, despondent, frustrated, look to the one who raised himself from the grave to raise you up and give you hope and help (Jn 11:25).

Jesus is the true vine. We must be connected to him for nourishment for life (Jn 5:1).

Jesus is king. When you need to appeal to a higher power, a greater authority, when you need clout, appeal to Jesus who reigns in majesty (Jn 18:37).

Jesus is the living water. When you are thirsty for something that will quench the thirst of life, to quell the longings, to handle the cravings that seem to overpower you, then look to Jesus, and his presence will bring refreshment (Jn 4:10).

Jesus is God. If you need forgiveness, grace, mercy and a fresh start in life, come to the author of life (Jn 13:19; 14:11, 20; 18:8).

If you have never read through the Gospels of Matthew, Mark, Luke and John, begin today. In your journal, record any verses that help you gain a clearer picture of Christ and give you strength for your journey. As you discover more about Jesus, you'll also discover you gain more peace.

10

$\mathscr{V}$ISION

"Reach high, for the stars lie hidden in your soul.
Dream deep, for every dream precedes the goal."
PAMELA VAULL STARR

$\mathscr{W}$hen JoeAnn Ballard was six months old, her parents divorced, and she and her siblings were sent to live with a foster family. JoeAnn's foster parents, Ora Mae and DeLoach Benjamin, provided her (and forty-eight other foster children!) with a loving, Christian home. It was in this loving home that the foundation of JoeAnn's future was laid. As a teen, JoeAnn went to a revival, and there she accepted the gospel message she had been raised on.

JoeAnn had a dream of going to Bible college, but her aging parents (then seventy years old) were apprehensive, knowing they might not be around to help her financially if the seemingly impractical Bible degree couldn't provide for her. JoeAnn comments, "I'm sure they were thinking, 'How is a black girl going to make a living going to Bible college?'"

One day while she was picking cotton, men dressed in suits came strolling on to the property. She thought they were buyers for her family's pea crop, but when she came out of the field in her bare feet, she soon discovered that one of the men was the president of a Bible college.

JoeAnn went to the Bible college, and at her graduation she was the only woman graduate. The leaders had no idea what to do with her—she had a degree, but no job and nowhere to go.

The third day after graduation, the leaders approached JoeAnn and asked her to go to Memphis. A church had closed there, and they needed JoeAnn to start a Sunday School. Her salary would be eighty dollars a month. Once in Memphis JoeAnn stayed with a pastor and his wife, paying them forty dollars a month for room and board and spending the other forty dollars on ministry. For six weeks she knocked on doors, cleaned the decaying church building, cut the grass—but no one came.

JoeAnn felt like giving up. "One day I sat on the piano stool and cried, 'I don't know what I am going to do. I can't go home. I feel like you've called me, Lord . . . but I don't know what to do.'"

Then the words of Isaiah 40:30-31 came to her mind:

> Even youths will faint and be weary,
>   and the young will fall exhausted;
> but those who wait for the LORD shall renew their strength,
>   they shall mount up with wings like eagles,
> they shall run and not be weary,
>   they shall walk and not faint. (NRSV)

As she pondered the challenge to wait upon the Lord, her hope returned. She began to see the neighborhood with new eyes. She saw the people were needy. But she wondered how she, a young woman with barely enough money for her own needs, was going to meet the needs of others. She felt God answering her, "Step in and I'll show you what I can do with five dollars." She decided to go to the thrift shore and buy as much as she could with her five dollars. JoeAnn shares what happened: "I loaded up my car with clothes. I gave the kids things to wear—and they started to come to Sunday School!"[1]

JoeAnn soon met and married Monroe Ballard, a man who shared JoeAnn's vision of helping others. While JoeAnn worked as a cashier and Monroe as an elementary school teacher, they continued to minister to the community around them. When they were asked by a church leader to help out a little girl in the neighborhood, the Ballards invited the little girl to their home for the weekend.

"Her hair was a mess, matted with gum," JoeAnn shares. "I combed her hair from Friday afternoon through Saturday at two o'clock. Over twenty-four hours combing hair!" But come Sunday morning, the little girl was clean, confident and well-fed both physically and spiritually, and the Ballards' vision for the future was becoming clearer. They began to bring more and more children over each weekend to give them food, clean clothes and a warm, safe place to sleep. Some of the children started staying longer than the weekends, and the Ballards decided to enlarge their tiny two-bedroom home.

For most women, raising their own children is a full-time job, but JoeAnn Ballard went a step further, showing love and compassion to every child she could. Today the Ballards have helped raised over 250 foster children, plus their own three biological children, and they have helped over fifteen of them attend Trevecca College.

JoeAnn's heart wasn't only for the children in her neighborhood, however. She had a vision to meet the needs of the poor and disadvantaged and share the gospel of Jesus Christ with them. One day she felt God calling her to put in her two weeks notice. JoeAnn shares what happened: "I left my job two weeks later with nothing planned. That afternoon, I heard about the Center."

The center she heard about was an urban ministry, started by Young Life and Campus Life in the back of a small inner city church. The center was looking for a leader, and when the call went out, the community naturally pointed to JoeAnn Ballard.

With JoeAnn as the director, the center grew to a dynamic charity operation with twenty branches in several cities. These centers, now called Neighborhood Christian Centers, offer daily food kitchens, family food pantries, clothes closets, rent and utility assistance, tutorial assistance, college scholarships, computer and job training, teen abstinence education, mentoring and self esteem programs, and various other Christian educational programs—all without the help of government financing. In Memphis alone over 125,000 families are helped each year.

Throughout her life, JoeAnn responded to God's call to pursue a vision of helping others: "God calls us to be our brother's keeper. I've taken hold of that call to do something about a person's situation rather than just sympathize with him." she adds.[2] She began to see the world through God's eyes. She saw a future where others had seen no hope, an opportunity where others saw obstacles, and potential where others saw disillusionment and decay.

Another Changed Life

Mary, too, is a woman who had a vision, a vision that has carried her from a childhood of poverty to a successful career in the banking industry.

As a child, Mary lived in Chicago's inner city, and by all accounts the cards were stacked against her even surviving to adulthood, let alone making anything of her life beyond the welfare rolls. Her parents struggled with addictions and depression, and Mary was moved from place to place, often from relative to relative. Often the basic necessities of food, clothing, shoes or even a roof over her head went unmet.

As a young woman Mary hit the streets in search of a job, going from place to place, to no avail. One day after walking out of yet another unsuccessful interview, she looked up into the vast Chicago skyline, where the huge familiar sign of the Bank of America building blinked out the time, day and temperature. *I'd love to work there someday, . . . but that will never happen.* Mary knew she had limited typing skills and a shy personality, so she let the hope evaporate from her mind and walked to the newspaper stand to see if there were any other job possibilities in the area. Opening the paper to the want ads, she scanned the page. A bank was hiring—*that bank!* "Something inside me urged me to go back into that bank building," Mary said to me. "I somehow knew it was the right thing to do."

She walked into the building she thought she'd never work in and got an interview for the position. In the interview, Mary was asked, "What are your career goals?" and when she meekly stated that she'd love to work in personnel management someday, the man interviewing her let out an uproarious laugh.

Mary landed a typist job that day, and she decided to be the best at anything she was given. She soon realized that education was a key to her future, so she enrolled in night courses. During this time, Mary also began to long for a deeper relationship with the God she had been taught about as a child. She found a church that could teach her more about

God and his Word, and she took steps to deepen her walk with God. She was baptized, and she attended classes and services where she discovered that God was her only source of strength and security.

"Who can say where a person can and cannot go?" Mary says. "As a child and young adult, I was constantly told I could not do certain things. I didn't have much hope of accomplishing things in life. I struggled because I had dreams but had no belief that I would ever achieve them. But I have come to know God as my provider. His word says in Psalm 37:4, 'Delight yourself also in the Lord, and he shall give you the desires of your heart.' I had a desire for a career."

If one door shuts, he'll open another. It's not a crisis; it's a change.

Today Mary is a vice president overseeing personnel for the Bank of America, and when people ask Mary how she handles the stress of the banking world with its constant takeovers, buyouts and downsizing, she shares the source of her strength and inner assurance with them.

I believe that God is my source. As I continue to delight myself in the Lord, I have been given such hope! I have seen many of my dreams fulfilled. I now have a happy marriage and a husband who has been a blessing in my life and the life of my son. I continue to be amazed at how awesome God is. His provisions are not just material things, they are in many areas. He cares for me! His love is complete, merciful and compassionate. I didn't just survive all the cutbacks, but continued to grow in my career. I see that as the hand of God, guiding me, preparing me. God holds my future. If one door shuts, he'll open another. *It's not a crisis; it's a change.* I'll be here as long as he wants, and then he'll move me on and it will be something good.

A Vision for You, a Vision for Others

JoeAnn and Mary had vision—the God-given ability to see things for what they could be rather than for what they are. They responded to his calling, opened their eyes and saw what God sees—hope, potential, opportunity. And when a person captures life from God's perspective, nothing can harness the visionary excitement. Nothing can stop the heart that's been power-packed by God.

When a person captures life from God's perspective, nothing can harness the visionary excitement.

Perhaps you are wondering how so many of the women in this book got the guts to step into their dreams and answer the call God had on their life. For me, it boils down to a few key questions.

Why not me? If I really believe God is as awesome as he is explained in the Bible, I should be stepping out in big ways for God. God wants me to think big, dream big and step into the best and broadest—unless he tells me something else. Henrietta Mears said, "There is no magic in small plans. When I consider my ministry, I think of the world. Anything less than that would not be worthy of Christ nor His will for my life."[3] I assume God needs leaders in all fields, and I see a leadership vacuum, largely because women have not believed God in their lives.

How do I prepare? The courage to act on your vision ultimately comes from God, but we must prepare our hearts and minds for the sometimes difficult tasks that accompany our dreams.

If there is a tug in your heart, capitalize on it in prayer. Before you leap into something—pray. Count the cost by praying and talking to people and take baby steps, little bitty steps. JOEANN BALLARD

First, prepare as a *person*. Deepen your walk with God by studying his Word and spending time in prayer. Find a mentor and ask her, "What did you do to prepare?" Then do all you can—get the education you need, the experiences and interning situations to learn the ropes, and discipline yourself. JoeAnn Ballard offers this advice: "God will give you insight to do his will. If there is a tug in your heart, capitalize on it in prayer. Before you leap into something—pray. Count the cost by praying and talking to people and take baby steps, little bitty steps."

Next prepare your *platform*. Place the props and structure in your life. For example, get your personal life in order at home. Be a great mom, wife and daughter. You may need your family as teammates later as God expands your platform. Get your living quarters set, create a productive routine, find a rhythm that allows for hard work—and for adequate R and R.

The next step is to prepare your *portfolio*. Be faithful in the little things. If you see something, do it—whether you will get the credit or not. Volunteer for opportunities that will add to your resume or expose you to new people and experiences. Keep samples of your work. Treat every person like a king, and you'll be given the opportunities of a queen.

Finally, prepare the *people*. The largest obstacle in pursuing your dreams is usually getting others to see the vision. Your family and friends need to see in you in a role long before you have the nameplate. Anyone who will be affected by your dream needs to be prepared for the dream come true. Share the dream so often and in so many ways that people naturally repeat it. The more you state the vision, the more the vision feels like it will become a reality.

Those who sacrifice for your dream need to be constantly thanked for their sacrifices. And as much as possible, don't allow those around you to suffer for the sake of your calling. For example, if I need to push to make a deadline, I try to still be mom and wife first. It isn't always a perfect balance, but having that as a goal helps me keep my highest priorities in order.

During a long building program at our church, my husband, Bill, repeated at every opportunity, "God will do through us, what is beyond us." God has big plans for all of us, and he wants us to lay hold of them. Begin preparing today to receive the vision he has for you. God's word will give you light so you can receive vision.

Winning Words

You are my lamp, O LORD; the LORD turns my darkness into light. The precepts of the LORD are right, giving joy to the heart. The commands of the LORD are radiant, giving light to the eyes. For with you is the fountain of life; in your light we see light. Send forth your light and your truth, let them guide me; let them bring me to your holy mountain, to the place where you dwell. Your word is a lamp to my feet and a light for my path. For it is light that makes everything visible.[4]

Winning Ways

The Gospel of Mark tells the story of a blind man out of hope. There was no vision for his life. The world around him saw no purpose for his life — they gave him only scorn and ridicule. They blamed his blindness on some unknown sin he must have committed. His blindness, they thought, was God's punishment.

> When he heard that it was Jesus of Nazareth, he began to shout, "Jesus, Son of David, have mercy on me!" . . .
> Jesus stopped and said, "Call him."
> So they called to the blind man, "Cheer up! On your feet! He's calling you." . . .
> "What do you want me to do for you?" Jesus asked him.
> The blind man said, "Rabbi, I want to see."
> "Go," said Jesus, "your faith has healed you." Immediately he received his sight and followed Jesus along the road. (Mk 10:46-52)

Jesus explained the real story: " 'Neither this man nor his parents sinned,' said Jesus, 'but this happened so that the work of God might be displayed in his life' " (Jn 9:3).

Sometimes it is difficult to envision a future for yourself or others. It may feel like hope is dead. But before you give up your vision, consider this story:

England, because it is an older country and it is small, started running out of places to bury people. So, they would dig up coffins and take their bones to a house and reuse the grave. In reopening these coffins, one out of twenty-five coffins was found to have scratch marks on the inside, and they realized they had been burying people alive. So they thought they would tie a string on their wrist and lead it through the coffin and up through the ground and tie it to a bell. Someone would have to sit out in the graveyard all night to listen for the bell. Hence on the "graveyard shift" they would know that someone was "saved by the bell" or he was a "dead ringer."

Could it be that God wants you to be one of the visionaries sitting by people that seem to be spiritually, socially, or emotionally "dead"? You may be the only one who hears the ringing in your heart. Your vision could be what God uses to give them the opportunity to be saved by the bell. Look for the potential in someone who is hard to love today. Ask God to give you this vision, this ability to see you, your life and those around you with *his* eyes. That vision may or may not change them, but it will change you!

11

$\mathscr{F}$OCUS

"To gain that which is worth having,
it may be necessary to lose everything else."
BERNADETTE DEVLIN

$\mathscr{H}$elen Duff Baugh is a woman of focus. Raised by parents with a strong faith, she grew up understanding that prayer, Bible teaching and evangelism were part of everyday life. Her mother was a talented Bible teacher and evangelist, and her father trained hundreds to be ministers on every continent in the world.

In the early 1900s, Helen's family decided to move from Ireland to America. Her father, Reverend Walter Duff, came to the states ahead of the family; he booked passage for them on the safest vessel of the day— the *Titanic*. However, Helen's mother, Mathilda, missed her husband so desperately that she changed the travel arrangements, and the family set sail two weeks earlier than expected. Helen, just a child herself, couldn't help but notice the providence of God as she heard the newspaper boy shout, "Extra! Extra! Titanic Sinks!"

When Helen was twelve, she came to know God in a personal way and began to sense his hand in her life. In her autobiography, *The Story Goes On*, she writes:

> While still in my teens I remember a community called Park Place near us where a lovely church was standing vacant, and I asked Father if we could

start a Sunday School there. Father agreed, and we went to check on the use of the building. As we discussed this with various people in the community, someone said, 'Why not let them go ahead? They are only young people and they can't do any harm.' So we started calling in every home in the community. Everyone was invited to Sunday School, and soon we had the place filled, not only with children but adults as well.[1]

This was just the beginning of ministry for Helen, a ministry that called her to rural communities that had church buildings in need of repair and people in need of leadership. Helen describes one church that stood out in her memory as "very dilapidated . . . the windows were all broken out, the door hanging open, and strange to say, the big pulpit Bible was lying open on the pulpit, its pages flipping back and forth in the wind." Helen was haunted by the picture of churches across the country in this neglected state, of towns vacant of the vital living hope of the gospel.

Soon the Duff sisters found themselves traveling through rural America, singing and planting Sunday schools, leading vacation Bible schools and engaging in other creative works. These pursuits often helped to strengthen a small, weary congregation that longed for the quality teaching and leadership the girls provided, and many times their ministry resulted in a new congregation that continued after they left.

The girls soon married. Helen wed a man named Elwood Baugh, a successful executive who had a big heart and who loved to use his talents and resources to serve God and others. Helen enjoyed domestic life in San Jose, California, but longed to do something eternally focused to bring Christ to her community. She began to pray with a new friend, the city manager's wife, and soon a prayer meeting developed every Monday morning. As she drove home, through a different neighborhood, she began to pray for this area of her community as well. Soon she met a woman in the area, and a prayer meeting on Monday afternoon fell into place. She contacted another friend in a different area of town, and a Tuesday group developed. Then Helen was asked to come to her husband's bank on Wednesdays to lead a prayer meeting for any employees who wanted to pray during lunch.

Soon twenty-four groups were meeting throughout San Jose for prayer meetings on different days of the week. Then on the first day of the month all the groups met together, with over one hundred showing up monthly to pray. Even after her children were born, Helen would rise early to get her home responsibilities done, and then she'd give her day to the Lord for his leading.

One evening, her husband presented Helen with a new ministry opportunity. Some of the single women working at his bank had many questions about God and were hoping Mr. Baugh could answer them. Mr. Baugh sensed it would be a wonderful opportunity for Helen to minister to the women, and so Elwood and Helen treated the women to dinner out while they answered their questions. It went so well that the women wanted to meet again the next week!

The meetings quickly became more formal, and the women decided to name the organization the Christian Businesswomen's Council. They elected officers, and the Baughs encouraged them to take on a ministry project—and what better project than rural American churches! Soon the ministry duplicated itself in other cities, and each of these groups committed to funding a team of young women ministering in a rural area.

One day Helen traveled with her children to Canon Beach, Oregon, to visit a ministry team there, leaving her beloved husband at home to work. During that trip, while at a dinner with her extended family, there was a knock on the door. It was a Western Union telegram telling Helen that Elwood had been killed in an accident.

Helen was shocked and grief-stricken. Elwood had been her greatest support. He had been her partner in the vision and the love of her life. What was she to do now? In desperation, she picked up the devotional she and Elwood had been reading on a daily basis. On the day of Elwood's passing, the Scripture read, "When thou goest, thy way shall be opened up before thee step by step." It was as if God had sent a personal message of hope, and a strange sense of peace enveloped Helen. She didn't know exactly how it was going to work out, but she knew God was calling her forward.

Helen accepted the fact that God had a plan for her without Elwood, and in time her grieving was replaced with a new focus. She courageously committed to stepping into a life of purpose—a life with her eyes off herself—as the leader of this new organization. It was going to take more focus than she had ever experienced, but she knew that God was faithful.

The work of the Christian Businesswomen's Council grew, and soon a new organization called Village Church Missions was formed by Helen's sister Evangeline and her husband Archie, in order to provide leadership for rural churches. Both organizations grew rapidly as the Christian Businesswomen's Council expanded their ministry to other professional women and also expanded the work of Village Church Missions by supporting the organization financially.

When many of the young professional women got married, they decided to form a new group in order to reach their friends with the good news of Jesus. As a result, Christian Women's Clubs were born. Husbands, too, wanted to use the same outreach-oriented format to reach couples, and soon several Professional Couples' Clubs were formed. Bible coffees for follow-up and discipleship naturally followed. And all these outreach ministries needed booklets and other written information, so a publishing company sprang up to meet the need. This burgeoning ministry needed a permanent home!

As in all decisions, Helen committed the need to prayer. She and her team decided to ask the Lord to provide the money for the need, and they were led to Stonecroft, a lovely brick home on many acres in the country outside Kansas City. When the papers were signed, the ministry agreed to pay at least $200 a month. Helen writes:

> From the very inception of this ministry, it was my policy that I would not send out letters asking for money. . . . We did let people know that we had bought the property and told them that only gifts earmarked for the purchase would be used that way. Soon the gifts began to arrive. . . . It was time to make our first payment, . . . so down to the bank went our bookkeeper with the checks. After handing the man a check for $200 for the first payment, she said, 'We'd like to give you this, too.' And she handed the man a check for $2,000!

The next month was the same—$200 with $2,000 extra. So the bank sent out a representative to ask the ministry to *slow down* repaying the loan!

Maintaining Focus

Focus is the ability to stick to a task regardless of the distractions. Focus clears a path where there has been none. Focus gives the fortitude to hang tough, to push through, to come back to the main thing and keep it the main thing. Focus is what keeps us on task and prevents our lives from drifting to mediocrity.

Any woman who wants to fulfill God's purpose in her life must make a commitment to maintain focus.

Helen knew what focus was. She was able to carry out God's unique calling in her life because she maintained focus on his purpose for her throughout her life. The ministry that began in her youth has now blossomed to an organization called Stonecroft Ministries, which now includes over a thousand staff members and spans a number of diverse ministries. As a result of Helen's focus, thousands of other people have discovered their God-given ministries. That is the way focus works: When you stay focused on God's calling in your life, you enable others to discover their calling as well.

Any woman who wants to fulfill God's purpose in her life must make a commitment to maintain focus. The everyday demands of life will try to steal your ability to focus. Life's setbacks will try to discourage you from completing the plan God has created uniquely for you. To get to the finish line of God's purpose for your life, you must have a plan to keep your desire high. I would like to recommend to you a number of ways to maintain focus in your life.

Look to the eternal. I have come to realize that life is longer than seventy or eighty years. It is eternal. Most of my life will take place in the presence of God, and nothing on earth can take that away from me. The important part of my life, then, is the investment I make in eternity. With this in mind, I often ask myself, *Is what I am doing today making an investment in eternity?* When I have to choose between two pressing needs, I ask, "Which has a more eternal focus?" Seeing life from this perspective enables me to keep my heart focused.

Look to the reward. Everyone will work harder if they know there is a reward. Ultimately our reward comes in eternity, but it helps to have smaller rewards along the way. A massage, a day off, a movie, a date with

Bill, fun with my three boys or a friend can keep me in focus. It is a like a small light at the end of the tunnel that reminds me of the bigger reward to come.

Look to the goal. Every woman has the uncanny ability to achieve whatever she focuses on. If we focus on our shortcomings or setbacks, we guarantee failure. If we focus on God's plan, we will fulfill his purpose. But keeping my goals in focus is a tough challenge, so I will often review the goals I have set and why they were important to me at the time. A short memory is the enemy of long-term goals!

Look to my cheerleaders. God has faithfully put people in my life who believe in my dream. They are not blind to my shortcomings, but they are highly supportive of God's calling in my life. Sometimes I have to go to them and ask them to help me say no to a very good thing that will be a distraction for me. They encourage me through prayer, phone calls, e-mail and face-to-face conversations. When I feel myself losing focus, I look to them for help.

Outward Focus with an Inward Leading

More than anything else, prayer keeps my heart focused. Prayer elevates me to a heavenly perspective and provides the desire and strength to see the vision become reality. The more in tune I am with God, the more I communicate with him, the more I am able to focus. And through prayer, God communicates to me the purpose he has for my life.

More than anything else, prayer keeps my heart focused. Prayer elevates me to a heavenly perspective and provides the desire and strength to see the vision become reality.

But sometimes we cannot hear God speaking to us. I believe Dallas Willard, in his book *Hearing God,* captures the true problem people face when they feel they are not hearing from God: "Perhaps we do not hear the voice of God because we do not expect it. Then again, perhaps we do not expect it because we know that we fully intend to run our lives on our own and have never seriously considered anything else."[2]

How easily we forget that "in him we live and move and have our being" (Acts 17:28)! Willard continues, "Generally speaking, God will not compete for our attention. . . . God will not run over us. We must be open to the possibility of God's addressing us in whatever way he chooses, or else we might walk right past a burning bush instead of saying as Moses did, 'I must turn aside and look at this great sight, and see why the bush is not burned up' (Ex. 3:3)."[3]

If you believe God has told you to do something, ask him to confirm it to you three times: through his Word, through circumstances, and through other people who may know nothing of the situation. JOYCE HUGGETT

Sometimes, though, we think we hear God, but because we are human, imperfect, fallible, we may not always hear, or receive, the message well. Joyce Huggett, a missionary and Christian author, gives this advice, "If you believe God has told you to do something, ask him to confirm it to you three times: through his Word, through circumstances, and through other people who may know nothing of the situation."[4]

As we grow in faith, God enables us to discern his voice more clearly. And when we cry out with a desire to live a life reflecting his character and calling, he answers. The book of Proverbs explains:

> If you call out for insight and cry aloud for understanding, and if you look for it as for silver and search for it as for hidden treasure, then you will understand the fear of the LORD and find the knowledge of God. For the Lord gives wisdom, and from his mouth come knowledge and understanding. (Prov 2:3-6)

> Trust in the Lord with all your heart and lean not on your own understanding; in all your ways acknowledge him, and he will make your paths straight. (Prov 3:5-6)

Good networkers are grateful and seek to give back to the people and places that helped them gain.

God clearly wants to communicate with you about his plan for your life. We are not required to manufacture our own purposes. We are simply called to listen to the calling of God.

And what is the result of a listening heart? Helen Duff Baugh could answer that. In an era when very few women led any organization, she answered God's call to lead, and her focus led to Stonecroft Ministries, which is now 1,800 groups strong, including Christian Women's Clubs, Christian Business and Professional Women, Village and Rural Missions Churches, After 5's, Couples' Clubs, One-Hour Groups and an assortment of Christian publications. There are over 1,600 local representatives, and more than 14,000 people are involved in various forms of leadership. The work of Stonecroft Ministries reaches all fifty states and sixty-one foreign countries.

One woman, with a heart for the unreached, listened to God's calling for her life and impacted thousands of people. If you focused on God's calling today, what could you do?

Winning Words

Jesus said to the woman, "Your faith has saved you; go in peace." I am the gate; whoever enters through me will be saved. And everyone who calls on the name of the Lord will be saved. Salvation is found in no one else, for there is no other name under heaven given to men by which we must be saved." We believe it is through the grace of our Lord Jesus that we are saved. Believe in the Lord Jesus, and you will be saved. Since we have now been justified by his blood, how much more shall we be saved from God's wrath through him! For if, when we were God's enemies, we were reconciled to him through the death of his Son, how much more, having been reconciled, shall we be saved through his life! That if you confess with your mouth, "Jesus is Lord," and believe in your heart that God raised him from the dead, you will be saved. For it is with your heart that you believe and are justified, and it is with your mouth that you confess and are saved . . . for, "Everyone who calls on the name of the Lord will be saved." But I pray to you, O LORD, in the time of your favor; in your great love, O God, answer me with your sure salvation.[5]

Winning Ways

Acts 1:8 says, "But you will receive power when the Holy Spirit comes on you; and you will be my witnesses in Jerusalem, and in all Judea and Samaria, and to the ends of the earth." The Spirit of God will empower you to reach your world with the hope and help of the good news of a personal relationship with Christ. But who is in your world? Focus on these three circles:

Your Jerusalem (your closest circle of friends and family). In your journal, list five people you will begin to pray for that they might come to know God personally.

Your Judea (your neighborhood, dorm, business circle, etc.). Begin to pray that God would show you one effective way to share your personal relationship with God to those you have something in common with.

Your Samaria (those you have zero in common with, you don't like, or may even be afraid to be seen with). Choose one people group that is hard for you to love and do something to help that group sense God's love for them. For example, give an at-risk kid a camp scholarship *and* take her to lunch, write her a note or send a gift package to her at camp. Don't worry about what to say or how to say it. God promises to meet you as you share him. Mark 13:11 says, "Do not worry beforehand about what to say. Just say whatever is given you at the time, for it is not you speaking, but the Holy Spirit."

12

*𝒞*OURAGE

"Heat is required to forge anything.
Every great accomplishment is the story of a flaming heart."
MARY LOU RETTON

*𝒯*hey call her Flo-Jo. America cheered for her as she ran down the track to gold, not once, not twice, but three times. Since then she's become a well-known speaker, actress and businesswoman.

Florence Griffith Joyner grew up in a Los Angeles housing project, one of eleven children raised by a single mother. Most people wouldn't have given her any hope, but Flo-Jo had courage to pursue her dreams. "I've always had this everlasting faith that has taught me that with faith, with belief in myself, and if I carry God everywhere I go," Flo-Jo says, "I'll be able to move mountains. And despite all the obstacles . . . I've never gone alone."[1]

People have commented on seeing Flo-Jo talk to herself at the starting line before a race. Flo-Jo explains:

> I wasn't talking to myself; I was asking Jesus, "Lord, stay right here. Don't make me the winner. Just give me the strength to do what you've given me to do, what I've practiced all my life for. And that's to do the best I can do. I don't care if I win or lose, as long as I give my best. And if my best is a gold medal, then yes, I would like the medal."

God answered Flo-Jo's prayer and gave her both courage and a medal, not once, but several times over.

Flo-Jo also had a desire to help others pursue their goals, so she started the Florence Griffith Joyner Youth Foundation, an organization that helps inner city youth discover the courage to follow their dreams. The students fill out goal cards, and the foundation seeks to provide them with the necessary information, financial support and everything else they need to make their dreams come true. "If we can take the pressure away from them and put them in a positive environment, it makes miracles," Flo-Jo says. "We just try to say, 'Hey, we love you. Tell us what you want to become.'"

No one else can run the race for you. FLORENCE GRIFFITH JOYNER

Flo-Jo encourages everyone to dream a little: "Set goals and write them down. Doing so will help you know where you want to go. . . . Make sure your goals are your goals. . . . No one else can run the race for you. See your goals every day: I have my goals and dreams posted in my house, on the refrigerator, in the garage, in the car—wherever I'm going to be throughout the day. Seeing is believing when you have faith. Never give up: It may take years to reach your goals. It took me 20 years to fulfill my dream [winning three Olympic gold medals]. But I knew sooner or later my dream would come true."

From Weary to Winner

Olympic courage isn't intrinsically born; it is cultivated. A young future Olympic hopeful grew up in the congregation where my husband and I pastor. Rachel Tidd, the sixth of ten children, started in gymnastics at seven, was a natural and learned quickly. At thirteen she decided she wanted to try for the Olympic team. She says, "Sometimes I used to think I wasn't as good as every one else, but I really wanted to go to the Olympics. Others told me I was so good, but I kind of doubted myself, but people kept telling me I had a chance, and now I believe I am as good as others who have this dream. I have a chance, too."

During Rachel's freshman year of high school, however, her love and passion for the sport was undermined by frequent injuries and mental stress caused by changes in coaching methods. One Sunday morning after church, Rachel and I talked and prayed for God's will and plan. I sensed she was physically, emotionally and spiritually drained, despite solid support from her caring parents and friends. That day I recognized in Rachel what I have seen in the eyes of so many other women and in myself on occasion—Rachel was weary. Maybe you've been there? I think we all get weary at times. Weary of pleasing others and fearing you might let them down. Weary of the chore of interpersonal relationships. Weary of the grind of the same thing day in and day out. Weary of being a woman who appears to have it all but is now too tired to enjoy it!

When I recognize this weariness in myself, I know that only in God's presence will my courage to continue pursuing my dreams be revived. This fall, I had weeks of back-to-back speaking engagements and media appearances. One night before a scheduled trip to Colorado, I attended my son's football game, and one of his friends whom he had led to Jesus was injured and had to be rushed to the hospital. My family and I went to the hospital to be with him, and at one o'clock in the morning, we were still there.

The next morning I had to rise at 4:30 a.m. in order to catch my flight, and I remember thinking, *Good, my flight got booked with some breathing space. I'll get there early, take a nap, shower and feel so refreshed.* No such luck. I arrived at the Denver airport only to discover that my connecting flight was cancelled, and I was stuck in the airport for five hours. I would have to dress for the event in the airport restroom and step off the plane into the pulpit. My heart sank. My body longed for a bed. How was I ever going to get the rest I needed stranded in an airport?

I walked through the terminal and prayed. I spotted an empty gate, one with a door that opened to the outside allowing fresh air to stream in. (This is a miracle in an airport!) I created my own lounge chair by placing my suitcase under my legs and my purse under my head and began to read a book by A. W. Tozer about the character of God. As I read, some birds hopped into the terminal and began to feed on the crumbs of tourist food, and I remembered the verse, "Look at the birds of the air; they do not sow or reap or store away in barns, and yet your heavenly Father feeds them. Are you not much more valuable than they?" (Mt 6:26). And for a moment in time, those birds reminded me of God's providence and care. I smiled, read the final page of my book and drifted off to sweet slumber—in the airport! (This could this be a modern version of Psalm 23:2-3: "He makes me lie down in green pastures, he leads me beside quiet waters, he restores my soul." I just never thought of an airport as a green pasture before!)

I awoke an hour later, safe, refreshed and thankful that those who wait on the Lord gain renewed strength and courage. On that day, the all-knowing God created a refreshing and memorable time just for me right in the middle of a crowded and chaotic airport. Too often we panic and chase after quick-fix solutions to our stress. All the while God is waiting for us to turn to him so he can give supernatural strength and courage to continue walking the path he has created for us: "Find rest, O my soul, in God alone; my hope comes from him" (Ps 62:5).

The courage to pursue our dreams is often directly linked to whether or not we believe God is trustworthy.

I knew that Rachel, too, would be renewed by God, so I strung together some verses that had boosted me with renewed courage and confidence. Then I gathered a small team of people to pray for Rachel. Rachel took a brief sabbatical to recover from a physical injury, all the while pondering the character of God and gaining renewed strength from his presence. When she returned to gymnastics, she was re-energized and quickly moved to the next level of competition.

At every meet Rachel has a team of people praying for her. And Rachel always carries a gift from her dad with her to each meet —a little card that simply says, "I can do all things through Christ who strengthens me" (Phil 4:13). She is now looking to gain a platform that would help her share her faith even more broadly—the coveted place on the Olympic team.

Count on It

In *The Wizard of Oz*, the tin man wanted a heart, the scarecrow wanted a brain, and the lion wanted courage. Courage is something we all want— we all need to face down the fears of life. Life is intimidating, and opportunities, even positive opportunities, can seem daunting, gigantic and insurmountable.

The courage to pursue our dreams is often directly linked to whether or not we believe God is trustworthy. But how can we know God is for real? How do we know he'll be there for us when we're depending on him? How can we know he'll keep the promises written in the Bible?

I like to go back to the first book of the Bible, to Genesis 15, my favorite chapter in the Bible. People often ask me, "Pam, why is this your favorite chapter in the Bible? How about the Beatitudes or 1 Corinthians 13, the chapter on love—why this one?"

It is my favorite chapter because all my courage for living comes from it. You see, in Genesis 15, God promises to make Abraham's offspring as many as the stars and to give him a homeland. But Abraham, like all of us, wanted reassurance that God's promises would come true, so God makes a covenant with Abraham. In biblical times, if someone wanted to make a covenant with another individual, they would cut animals in two and place the halves opposite each other. Then they would link their arms together and walk through the blood of the animals. It was their way of saying, "If I break my part of the bargain, you can do to me what we've done to these animals." A covenant was not to be taken lightly. You couldn't just hire some high-power lawyer, find a loophole and get out of it. It was a life and death commitment.

All my courage in life comes because I recognize God will never fail to keep his promises.

The covenant between God and Abraham was a little different, though. God knew Abraham was a fallible human being, incapable of keeping his part of the bargain forever, so God put Abraham to sleep and walked through the animals in a the form of a smoking firepot with a blazing torch. *God made a covenant with himself.* This means that if God fails to keep his promise, he will cease to exist. But we know God is eternal; he will always exist (Rev 4:8). Therefore, we can conclude that since God will *never* die, he will *always* keep his promises! All my courage in life comes because I recognize God will never fail to keep his promises.

God's promises will give you courage too. Courage to look yourself
square in the mirror and not blame anyone else for the mental stress you
are under (even if it is their fault!). Courage to take the situation and
place it in God's hands and allow his presence to wash over your soul to
renew your strength. Courage to face down a fear and develop a resolve
to see a dream through. Courage that explodes into determination, a
determination that forges a call and a character into the passion that can
carry you into the winner's circle—God's winner's circle of women of
confidence.

Winning Words

*Have I not commanded you? Be strong and courageous. Do not be terrified; do not be
discouraged, for the LORD your God will be with you wherever you go. The LORD
himself goes before you and will be with you; he will never leave you nor forsake you.
Do not be afraid; do not be discouraged. Rise up; this matter is in your hands. We
will support you, so take courage and do it. Be strong and very courageous. Be care-
ful to obey all the law my servant Moses gave you; do not turn from it to the right or
to the left, that you may be successful wherever you go. Turn your ear to me, come
quickly to my rescue; be my rock of refuge, a strong fortress to save me. For you
have been my refuge, a strong tower against the foe. O Sovereign LORD, my strong
deliverer, who shields my head in the day of battle. The name of the LORD is a strong
tower; the righteous run to it and are safe . . . for their Defender is strong; he will
take up their case against you. Finally, be strong in the Lord and in his mighty
power. Put on the full armor of God so that you can take your stand against the
devil's schemes. And the God of all grace, who called you to his eternal glory in
Christ, after you have suffered a little while, will himself restore you and make you
strong, firm and steadfast. I write to you, fathers, because you have known him who
is from the beginning. I write to you, young men, because you are strong, and the
word of God lives in you, and you have overcome the evil one. In all these things we
are more than conquerors through him who loved us.[2]*

Winning Ways

Have you ever needed courage and didn't know where to go? Read
Hebrews 11, the Hall of Fame of the courageous. Choose one courageous soul and do a character study of that person. In your journal,

answer these questions:

What was the obstacle to overcome?

How did he/she overcome?

What can you glean from his/her life and apply to your own?

13

CREATIVITY

"You pay God a compliment by asking great things of Him."
TERESA OF ÁVILA

LeeAnn Truesedale rejected the notion of God. LeeAnn, a bright dental student pursuing a masters in bio-chemistry, wanted to rise to the top in her chosen field, and God would only be a millstone around her neck, or so she thought. After all how could any scientist embrace creation? Weren't all bright, forward-thinking scientists those who only entertained theories of evolution? Creation just seemed too emotional, too experiential for her to believe, even though she really hadn't investigated it for herself. Time spent investigating seemed silly to her when all the professors and scientists she respected seemed to reject creation and the God who would be its "intelligent designer."

Then one day, new evidence landed in the lap of this aspiring dentist—evidence brought into play by her new lab partner, Terry. "I had never had anyone stand up to my arguments against the existence of God," remembers LeeAnn.

> From the very beginning of my friendship with Terry, he made it clear that his relationship with God was first and foremost. Not only that, he had the audacity to suggest that every word of the Bible was fact, even creation.

I was sure that no credible scientist, holding a doctorate degree from a respectable university, believed in scientific creationism. Terry brought me A. E. Wilder Smith's *The Creation of Life*, and the Josh McDowell books *Reasons Skeptics Should Consider Christianity* and *Evidence That Demands a Verdict*.

At this point, he had my attention; thus the debating began. To make a long story short, I was unable to prove to myself that evolution was true, especially in light of the huge problems with the fossil record. I could not reconcile the theory of evolution with the Second Law of Thermodynamics, nor with the faulty mathematics upon which evolutionary radiocarbon dating is based.

After several months, I began to look at the possibility that there was some type of Supreme Being, but wasn't ready to call him God or say that he had anything to do with me. After all, I was independently happy in my life. Soon thereafter, while procrastinating in writing my master's thesis in biochemistry, I began to read the book *More Than a Carpenter*. The words did not impact me at first, but did cause some degree of questioning. Things changed when I got to Josh McDowell's testimony [a lawyer trying to disprove Christianity]. I ended up in tears, on my knees, praying, *I don't know if You are there or not, but if You exist and know that I'm talking to you, I want to learn about You. Just let me know in some way that You are real*, and then I prayed asking Jesus into my heart.[1]

Examine the Evidence

LeeAnn had the mistaken belief that no credible scientists believed in God as creator. She was missing out on one of the greatest privileges of life until she began to examine the evidence. For me, the evidence of God's existence and creative wealth gives me confidence. And when I am confident, I am more creative. LeeAnn shares how a good look at the evidence put her in touch with her Creator:

> Many of the greatest scientists of the past were creationists and for that matter, were also Bible-believing Christians, men who believed in the inspiration and authority of the Bible, as well as in the deity and saving work of Jesus Christ. . . . And somehow this attitude did not hinder them in their commitment to the "scientific method." In fact one of them, Sir Francis Bacon, is credited with formulating and establishing the scientific

method! They seem also to have been able to maintain a proper "scientific attitude," for it was these men (Newton, Pasteur, Linnaeus, Faraday, Pascal, Lord Kelvin, Maxwell, Kepler, etc.) whose researches and analyses led to the very laws and concepts of science which brought about our modern scientific age.[2]

The evidence of God's existence and creative wealth gives me confidence.

The evidence of God's genius and creativity is abundant. The psalmist spoke nothing but truth when he wrote, "The heavens declare the glory of God; the skies proclaim the work of his hands" (Ps 19:1). Astrophysicist Hugh Ross shows a glimpse of our great Creator-God as he weaves the tapestry of the Bible together:

1. God existed before the universe. God exists totally apart from the universe, and yet can be everywhere within it (Gen 1:1, Col 1:16-17).

2. Time has a beginning. God's existence precedes time (2 Tim 1:9, Tit 1:2).

3. Jesus Christ created the universe. He has no beginning and was not created (Jn 1:3, Col 1:16-17).

4. God created the universe from what cannot be detected with the five senses (Heb 11:3).

5. After his resurrection Jesus could pass through walls in his physical body, an evidence of his extra-dimensionality (Lk 24:36-43, Jn 20:26-28).

6. God is very near, yet we cannot see him, a further evidence of his extra-dimensionality (Ex 33:20, Deut 30:11-14, Jn 6:46).

7. God designed the universe in such a way that it would support human beings (Gen 1 & 2, Neh 9:6, Job 38, Ps 8:3, Is 45:18).[3]

Is your mind expanding? Are you starting to realize that God has more to show you than you could ever come up with on your own? No one created God. God is the Creator who knows all, sees all and orchestrates all. He spoke the world into existence, and his existence is not dependent on the universe. Our minds can never fully comprehend his creative majesty.

Recently, on a flight home from a speaking engagement, I sat next to a woman who was crocheting complex tablecloths, knotting fine lace together with intricate stitches. The pattern was complex, yet she worked with ease. Her handiwork reminded me of Psalm 139, which says we are fearfully and wonderfully made, that we were knit together in the womb. Here is a glimpse into just how complex the human mind is:

> The adult brain weighs about 1350 grams, just three pounds, yet it handles the information of 1000 supercomputers . . . Note that the potential brain capacity is estimated as at least equivalent to that of 25 million volumes, a 500-mile-long bookshelf! Clearly, the brain is far more advanced than any computer ever produced.[4]

What's even more amazing is that we, as human beings, are created in the *image* of God. In their book *Why America Doesn't Work*, Chuck Colson and Jack Eckerd explain that because we were made in the likeness of God, and God is the ultimate Creator, we too long to create. Therefore, work itself is sacred:

> The reformers saw all work—sacred and secular, intellectual and manual—as a way of serving God. . . . What mattered was that each individual understood his or her calling or vocation; in that way they collaborated with God in the grand design of the universe, working for his glory, the common good, and their own fulfillment."[5]

The meaningful work God called you to pursue is your creative expression. The more creative you can be in your unique calling, the more enjoyable it will be for you, and the more it will challenge others to be their best.

Designed to Make a Difference

As LeeAnn came to know God the Creator, she was led to use her abilities and talents in creative ways that would positively impact others. Lee-Ann combined her scientific background with God's compassionate eyes for our world and became a creative advocate for children's health care issues:

> For many years I had been a member of the Junior League, an international women's and children's advocacy group which promotes professional volunteerism. I had also been very involved professionally serving

as a state delegate to the Nevada Dental Association, until being elected in 1995 to a four-year term as Officer of the Southern Nevada Dental Society, culminating in my Presidency in 1998-1999. [She was the second woman ever to hold this position.]

LeeAnn also became very active in indigent dental care, working on a project to advocate in favor of public water fluoridation in southern Nevada. LeeAnn shares this story about her work:

The project was the natural merging of my interests in indigent dental care, child advocacy, professional leadership and political activism. God used a major trial in my life and has made "all things work for good." In a nutshell, I became good friends with the partners of a law firm in the course of defending myself in the breakup of the purchase of a dental practice. When the firm later approached me regarding their interest in donating pro bono work on a child advocacy project, I suggested that they get involved with the fluoridation effort that I recently had presented to the Junior League Board of Directors. Both the Junior League of Las Vegas and the law firm accepted the challenge, making the passage of AB 284, the water fluoridation initiative (which places the proven safe and effective cavity-preventing fluoride in public drinking water) their pro bono project for 1999.

With their backing, as well as many other state and local organizations, our grassroots efforts paid off in last spring's legislative session, where I was blessed to testify before the joint committees of the Nevada State Senate and the House of Representatives, on behalf of both the Junior League of Las Vegas (as their appointed Senior Legislative Representative) and the Southern Nevada Dental Society (as their elected President). He also allowed me to be the representative voice for both the dentists and the child advocacy agencies of Southern Nevada. There are details of my scientific background that were so intimately tailored to the lines of questioning I was given by both the politicians and the opponents of the legislation, that it *had* to be God's doing. The end result was that the governor signed the bill into law. On March 1, 2000, the Southern Nevada Water Authority began regulating the fluoride levels to optimal.

When the legislation passed, LeeAnn saw the answer to a six-year prayer and her desire to create a life that would reflect God's glory.

My prayer was simply: *God, if You want to use me, I'll do whatever You want me to do. I only ask that You make it really obvious to me, so that I know it is what You want, and not just my own desires.* I had no idea that God would allow a litigation problem to bring me into contact with the people that would make this dream a reality. The involvement of both the Junior League and the law firm was critical, and for some strange reason, God allowed me to be the connector that brought the two organizations together. In hindsight, it seems as if God put me in *exactly* that place, at that time, to accomplish his plan.

Connect with the Creator

As you discover God's unique plan for you, he allows you to have a part in creating your future. Knowing that the possibilities are endless is exhilarating, but being creative does not always come easily. I know this true for me. Creativity is demanded in my chosen career, and thinking outside the box is an expected skill. I find the discovery of new ideas to be exciting, and I get a thrill when words come together to inspire others. But the constant need for creativity can be exhausting, and the well can run dry. So when life seems like the same old, same old, how can we get the creative juices flowing?

God is the greatest source of creativity available to us. When I need an infusion of creativity, I fix my gaze on my Creator.

I have found that God is the greatest source of creativity available to us. He is all-knowing, all-powerful, all-loving, all-just, all-*everything*! When I need an infusion of creativity, I fix my gaze on my Creator. Here are a few activities that keep me connected to God's creative influence.

Rest. God created the world in six days, and then he rested! Some of my best creative moments happen while I am resting—in the middle of the night, when I first wake up, as I am laying in a hammock, floating on a raft in the pool or playing a game with one of my children.

Spiritual discipline. The disciplines of solitude, silence, prayer and writing a personal journal give my soul white space, a clean slate for fresh ideas. When I am under a tight deadline, I *increase* my prayer time. I pray and ask God to unleash and anoint my creativity. I also look for worship music by artists who cause my mind to focus on the strength and power of God. Worshiping the Creator releases creativity. It is as if looking into the face of God expands my mind so new thoughts can enter.

Exercise. A hard workout releases endorphins which usually causes my creativity to flow. A walk, a dance or satisfying sex with my husband will provide the needed change of pace that jars loose new ideas.

Something new. I try to rub elbows with new or unique people or go to unique places on a regular basis. Good conversations with good friends produce a new flow of creative words for me. New experiences shared with others create memories that give birth to creative expression. I know I will never get to the end of all that God has put in this world, so these new experiences expose me to a little bit more of God's creativity.

In finding God and deepening your relationship with him, you gain access to his limitless creativity. LeeAnn and the other women in this book are confident of this because they have seen God's power and his amazing ability to create a solution for whatever situation you might be in. If you are willing, he will create new opportunities for you as he bolsters your confidence in his abilities—opportunities that will maximize your creativity and the impact it can have on your world.

Winning Words

His wisdom is profound, his power is vast. Who has resisted him and come out unscathed? He moves mountains without their knowing it and overturns them in his anger. He shakes the earth from its place and makes its pillars tremble. He speaks to the sun and it does not shine; he seals off the light of the stars. He alone stretches out the heavens and treads on the waves of the sea. He is the Maker of the Bear and Orion, the Pleiades and the constellations of the south. He performs wonders that cannot be fathomed, miracles that cannot be counted. When he passes me, I cannot see him; when he goes by, I cannot perceive him. Can you fathom the mysteries of God? Can you probe the limits of the Almighty? They are higher than the heavens—what can you do? They are deeper than the depths of the grave—what can you know? Their measure is longer than the earth and wider than the sea. He unleashes his lightning beneath the whole heaven and sends it to the ends of the earth. After that comes the sound of his roar; he thunders with his majestic voice. When his voice resounds, he holds nothing back. God's voice thunders in marvelous ways; he does great things beyond our understanding. He says to the snow, "Fall on the earth," and to the rain shower, "Be a mighty downpour." So that all men he has made may know his work, he stops every man from his labor. When I consider your heavens, the work of your fingers, the moon and the stars, which you have set in place, what is man that you are mindful of him, the son of man that you care for him? You made him a little lower than the heavenly beings and crowned him with glory and honor. The heavens declare the glory of God; the skies proclaim the work of his hands.[6]

Winning Ways

Have you ever felt like you needed to jump-start your creativity? No doubt you have. Tap into God's unlimited creativity through prayer and the study of his Word. Try expanding your view of God by reading a book by Phillip Johnson, Duane Gish, Henry Morris or Hugh Ross. Rest, pray, go for a walk, then sit down with your journal and ask God to help in an area of life where you feel stalled.

14

$\mathscr{E}$NDURANCE

"Faith isn't the ability to believe long and far into the misty future.
It's simply taking God at His Word and taking the next step."
JONI EARECKSON TADA

$\mathscr{I}$t all began with a note:

> Please help this boy. His father is a drunk. His mother is a whore. Mother
> has left home, he needs help. Look at what his mother did to him.

Soon after reading these words, Grace and Steve Cabalka were sitting in
a Romanian orphanage, waiting to meet the little boy they hoped to bring
back to the United States for medical help, and if possible, adopt. Grace
writes of their first meeting:

> Mario came in and with barely an audible whisper said, "Bunazia" (good
> day), gave us a kiss and very meekly sat on Steve's lap. He stayed about an
> hour. That night I wrote in my journal, *Mario seems so sweet. His hair and
> complexion seem undernourished, his eyes look dull . . . as all the kids here do. They
> have no life, nothing to look forward to. I found myself reserved toward him because he
> is not released to us yet. I had noticed that his clothes were 3 sizes too small and dirty,
> that he had burn marks on his legs and his left foot was turned out at a 90 degree
> angle. I remember noticing a patch of eyelashes was missing and there were several
> other scars as well. I wondered how long it would take him to heal from the emotional
> scars within.*[1]

Grace and Steve knew that God had called them to adopt Mario and were aware that many challenges lay ahead of them. Their three other children would have to adjust to his presence in their home. People would ask them over and over again if they were sure about what they were doing. And there would be years of emotional and physical healing to endure. But the biggest challenge of all would be working with the Romanian government.

At first, Grace thought the process would be straightforward and relatively efficient. Their goal was to get everything done in two businesses day. The courts would be open until two o'clock each day. "All we had left to do was go to court, get a birth certificate, get a passport, obtain a Visa, get signatures of release from some authorities, buy airline tickets . . . and we had fourteen hours to do it!" mused Grace.

"That afternoon," recalls Grace, "Steve called the American Embassy to confirm an appointment on Tuesday morning to have a visa issued for Mario. He also asked if there was anything they could do to help us get a court appearance. The embassy couldn't believe we hadn't even been to court yet, and that we were still expecting to get a visa on Tuesday! She laughed, 'You should expect to wait three to four months for a court appearance.'"

That night Mario was able to stay with Grace and Steve. It was that night that Grace began to recognize the long process of parenting that was ahead for them once they settled the legal issues. Grace compassionately related, "That night I remember teaching him how to hold my hand, how to bend his fingers across mine. He was unfamiliar with the simplest forms of mothering—tying his shoes, helping him change shirts. I prayed God would help him accept the love that would be waiting for him in our family."

At the same time Grace and Steve were struck with the need to pray desperately for Mario's release and for endurance to complete this journey. "At this point, Steve and I were experiencing the same emotions we would if we were intervening on behalf of one of our own biological children," remembers Grace. "I believe the Lord orchestrated those emotions in us to give us the stamina to keep going, to keep pushing, to never give up. Were we crazy? Did we really think we could get everything done in two business days?"

Prayer, at this point, seemed to be the most sensible approach. They

needed God to work for them. They needed to work hard with the time
they had available. They needed wisdom to know exactly what to do. As
they prayed specifically about getting through the court system smoothly
on Monday, their friend DeAnn had an idea: "Take pictures of Mario's
feet!"

On Monday, everyone went into action. Stamped documents needed
to be picked up at the police station, and they were to meet their lawyer,
Elena, at 8:30 a.m. to coordinate their efforts. They had to wait at the
police station for forty-five minutes while Marianna, their Romanian
advocate, secured the documents. They rushed to the courthouse, but by
the time they arrived, their lawyer was gone. She had left a message that
she would be back at 1:00 p.m., if she had time. "Thoughts raced though
my head," said Grace. *"What? If she has time! We had a 12:30 court date.
What about our court date? Did she reschedule? Why didn't she go in without us?"*

What happened next was an adventure they will never forget:

All day I was begging God to bring Elena back to the courthouse. At 1:15
she still wasn't there. We started talking about going in and pleading our
case without her. DeAnn, being an encourager, kept saying, "You can do
it, Grace. Go in there and fight for your son!" Steve and I began looking
over the documents, preparing to go in. Then Elena walked up!

We followed Elena and Marianna upstairs. They entered a door and disappeared for two hours. I walked away from the door and fell face down
on the floor. My legs gave out. I sobbed. I was not politely asking the Lord
for help, nor was I claiming his promises, I was begging God, from the
depths of my inner being, to free Mario. In the corridor that afternoon, all
of us felt Satan's cloud above us. We stood there, cried, prayed, and
begged God to intervene. Then we'd have silence, each one communing
with God independently, and then someone would start singing a praise
song and we'd all join in. I thought of how Peter sang in prison and how
God opened the prison doors. Every once in a while, someone would open
the door to the courtroom, and we'd peek in. The place was packed, and
ours was the last case to be heard. At 3:00, the judge, in his robe, walked
out of the courtroom, and Elena and Marianna followed him out. He was
leaving. Court adjourns at 3:00, and it was 3:00!

"Follow him, Steve!" DeAnn shouted. Elena whisked by us. "Where are you going?" I asked. She told Laura they were in the wrong courtroom! I thought, *Wrong courtroom! It took two hours to figure that out? Now court is closing? Now what?!*

Elena proceeded to run around the courthouse. We had no idea what she was doing; we weren't even sure what we needed the court to approve. We had to trust in God. The whole thing was so confusing. After several minutes, Elena ran up to us and told us to give her $3.00 to pay a secretary to type a document. Elena found a judge, a friend of hers, willing to handle our case outside of court and needed the secretary to type up the document. Elena was so excited. We ran over to the mayor's office to get the birth certificate but told her we wanted to meet her for dinner that night.

We arrived at Anna's office at 3:30 but had to wait. Several of the staff were arguing over what had to be done next. I thought we were done, what else did they need? One more paper, with one more stamp! It was a paper Marianna had to sign, so back to the orphanage we went to get the stamp!

Finally, we had everything Anna needed to draw up the birth certificate. DeAnn asked Anna if she would call her friend in the passport office like she had done for them earlier in January. It was 4:15 and the passport office closed at 4:30. Anna tried to call—but the lines were dead. She wrote out a quick note and off we went.

Standing at the locked gate of the passport office were two guards with machine guns. As we approached they asked us what we wanted. Marianna searched though her purse, because she had grabbed the note—there was no note! The office was closed, and we'd have to return in the morning. Marianna felt very bad. We set our plan for the morning in place. DeAnn and I would go to the passport office and Steve to the embassy. The type of visa we were requesting was only processed in the morning, and if we didn't make it by noon we'd be stuck again.

We all arrived at our destinations by 7:30 a.m. At the passport gate, we told the guards we were looking for Nicolea, Anna's friend. We were led to his office, talked with him briefly and were told to wait—and sat and waited nearly two hours! Finally, our translator went in the office to find out how long it would take and was told the meeting finished an hour before. We prayed, then sent Laura in with a gift of cheap cologne for him and for Nicolea's wife, a bottle of Pic-n-Sav perfume. They were our last two gifts—and it worked!

Within thirty minutes we had a passport in hand. We arrived at the Embassy a little past 11 a.m. Steve told us they had been extremely busy all morning and had stopped taking requests at 11 a.m. However, our counsel did agree to meet with us. He seemed irritated, peering over his glasses at us, asking questions with a discriminating eye. We showed him pictures of Mario, and he seemed more interested. He had all the documents with the senators' and congressmen's signatures, but he still gave us the third degree. However, within twenty minutes later we had the visa stamped inside Mario's passport.

Our final stop was the airline. We thought this would be no problem, but the flight was full! We shot up a prayer, and God sent us a woman in authority to hear our story. She okayed the purchase of a ticket.

We all met for a victory dinner. Elena loved meeting Mario. I'll never forget what she said about all that we had accomplished that week: "Beyond human power!"

Breaking Barriers

By consistently trusting and believing in God, Grace and Steve were able to stay on course. He gave them the strength and endurance to finish their journey, despite the obstacles that stood in their way. Like Grace and Steve, we, as women who lead, are often called by God to embark upon journeys that are fraught with numerous challenges and barriers. But breaking barriers is not for the faint of heart or the uninformed.

When I need a model for forging ahead into hostile territory, I turn to John 4:6-42 and glean from Christ's interaction with the Samaritan woman at the well. In his decision to enter Samaria and talk with this particular woman, Jesus broke down some of the most formidable barriers that exist in society.

Racial/ethnic barriers. During the time of Christ, Jews thought of Samaritans as second-class citizens, half-breeds and apostates. If you were traveling from the Galilean region in the north (Nazareth, Cana, Capernaum, etc.) to Jerusalem in the south, the most direct route would be straight through Samaria. However, Jews would add another day of travel just to go around Samaria instead of through it because they didn't want to tarnish their reputations by associating or even coming in contact with this despised group of people. Jesus did not let this barrier deter him from carrying out God's eternal plan to make disciples of all nations. Instead, he and his disciples went directly through Samaria and ministered to the people of that nation.

Gender barriers. In this time in history, women were seen as property, and most women never had the opportunity for education. But Christ affirmed that women have equal value in God's eyes. He often engaged in teaching conversations with women, like he did with the Samaritan woman at the well.

Class barriers. The woman at the well wasn't exactly the mayor of the community. She wasn't serving on the city council. She wasn't even prominent at the women's bridge club. She was going to get water at the well, doing servant's work. But Jesus did not think himself better than her; rather, he freely engaged her in conversation.

Piety barriers. Not only was the Samaritan woman doing servant work, she was not even a moral woman. She had had five husbands and was living with another man who was not her husband. Christ knew it, but he never shied away from sinful people.

The Samaritan woman lacked much in life, but what she did have, that most people lack, was a hunger and thirst for the truth. She longed for God and desired a relationship with him (see Jn 4:15-28). She knew she had a need only God could fill. She'd tried everything else.

Let the Walls Come Down

Little by little, Jesus broke down the barriers between the Samaritan woman and himself. But how? What steps did he take to overcome society's norms and reach out to the Samaritan people?

Build vision. Christ had an eternal mission, and men's agendas and politics were not part of it. Jesus had limited time on earth to carry out his task, and he didn't have time to be sidetracked by the barrier that the Jewish society had constructed with the Samaritan people. Instead, he focused on the plan God the Father had for his life.

If I keep my focus on serving God, he will remove barriers in my life.

I have found that if I keep my focus on serving God, he will remove barriers in my life. I have been the first white woman speaker in large African American, Asian American and Hispanic churches, not because I set out to do so but because the message God asked me to share struck a common chord in those dedicated women. I have been asked to address crowds of male audiences, finding myself as the only "skirt" on the platform, not because I am carrying a sign for gender equality but because I have chosen to pick up my cross and follow Jesus. I serve on boards where I am the only woman in a room full of men, not because I am engaged in any gender war but because I am concerned about winning hearts to God.

As we serve God, God will make a path for more service. By keeping my eye on the eternal goal, I can't see the people around me who are telling me I can't do something. I fix my eyes on him who is the author and perfecter of my faith, and I see what I am called to do. As I do it, cultural barriers fall.

It is exciting to see gender barriers topple so women are free to say yes to service to God in whatever area of calling he has for them. But those barriers will only continue to come down if we keep our focus on the greater good, not our personal victory. An "I told you so" attitude will slam the door shut, but a heart that continually asks, like the apostle Paul, "Am I now trying to win the approval of men, or of God? Or am I trying to please men?" (Gal 1:10) will consistently open doors of opportunity. We will gain more ground if we reflect Christ's mission and vision: Jesus said, "I seek not to please myself but him who sent me" (Jn 5:30).

Build relationships. Christ focused on building relationships with key people who had a heart for God. He poured his energies into building a community with his disciples and shared everything he knew of God with them. Because they knew Jesus was giving his all for them, they were loyal to him—even when he endangered their reputations by taking them through places like Samaria. They followed him even when he spelled out the cost, challenging them to "pick up your cross and follow me." Eventually the relationship meant so much to those disciples they would give their life for the call.

Jesus didn't lead from an ivory tower; he led by walking just a step ahead. I am not a very tall woman, so in crowds my husband will extend his hand to me. I will hold on to him and follow his broad shoulders as we swim upstream in a throng. I can't see the destination, but I can see him. In the same way, we give people confidence when we walk just ahead of them and extend a hand of training out to them. I never want to distance myself from those who I am passing the torch to. At a leadership conference, I heard Howard Hendricks so aptly say, "He who calls himself a leader but has no followers is simply taking a walk!"

Jesus also knew that to reach the world, he had to reach the hearts of those closest to him. He and his disciples ate together, traveled together, ministered together, constantly strengthening their relationship.

Sometimes we can lose sight of the people in the midst of running the program. I work at carving out one-to-one time with my team, using hidden snatches of time to keep relationships strong. E-mailing prayers and praise for a job well done, cell phone calls of encouragement or concern, "thinking of you" notes scribbled on postcards from far away cities are a few of the small things I do to keep relationships growing amidst the frantic pace of leadership life.

Thanking the people who support us is another important part of building relationships. Every year for Thanksgiving, each person in our family gets to invite a family to our home for a Wednesday pre-Thanksgiving meal by candlelight. At that dinner, we thank those families that have been an encouragement to us. We light the candle we have placed at each of their plates and give them a blessing, recognizing that our ability to make our goals is directly related to their involvement and influence in our lives.

Build bridges. Christ sought to build bridges with the people around him. He looked for the best, most fertile hearts, which often came packaged in the most unlikely persons. When we are seeking to create a path from one heart to another, from one thinking pattern to another, from one culture to another, we should seek to build a bridge.

But building bridges it not always an easy task. Consider the story of the Golden Gate Bridge in California. The concept of bridging the vast Golden Gate Strait was proposed as early as 1872 by railroad entrepreneur Charles Crocker. It was not until 1916, however, that the idea of a bridge was revived by James Wilkins, newspaper editor of the *San Francisco Call Bulletin*. Wilkins began an editorial campaign for a bridge which caught the attention of San Francisco City Engineer Michael M. O'Shaughnessy. O'Shaughnessy began a national inquiry among engineers regarding the feasibility and cost of such a project. The majority of engineers said a bridge could not be built. Some speculated it would cost over $100 million. However, Joseph Baermann Strauss, a designer of nearly 400 spans, said such a bridge was not only feasible, but could be built for only $25 to $30 million. Strong opposition continued even after construction began. The famous bridge was finally completed in 1937, sixty-five years after it was first proposed. Most bridges of change are like that—hard won, time consuming, energy intensive—and worth it!

How do you start? Look for a person who is also seeking to build a bridge. The Samaritan woman at the well was looking for ways to worship God. When Christ offered her living water, she was eager to hear more of Jesus had to say. Many of the strides in race relations are made because two people from opposing sides are seeking a common goal. They are looking to build a bridge to relationships with people who share the dream, regardless of ethnic origin.

Look for common ground. Maybe you don't agree on everything, but what do you agree on? Build on those things. I serve on the board of several interdenominational organizations. We have the ability to pull people from all kinds of backgrounds together because instead of traversing down all kinds of theological trails that might lead to differences, we focus on the theological principles we all agree upon.

Jesus and the Samaritan woman didn't have a lot of apparent common ground. The differences were enormous. He was a Jew, she a Samaritan. He was holy, she was wicked. He was a teacher, she uneducated. At the time, he was respected, she was scorned in her society. But Jesus was tired and thirsty, and the woman had a jug to draw water. The woman was thirsty spiritually, and Jesus could give her the living water. By using water as the common ground, he drew the woman into a spiritual conversation.

From there he used the natural ebb and flow of a conversation to build a bridge between them. He didn't condemn her or focus on her shortcomings but treated her with respect. He won over her heart, and she convinced everyone in her town to meet Jesus, the Messiah.

Step by Step

Breaking down barriers by building vision, relationships and bridges is a lifelong process, and more often than not, you will face resistance. You may have doubts within yourself, others may have doubts about what you are doing, circumstances may be daunting, but in your heart you know that the goals you are pursuing are what God designed you for and your heart tells you to continue despite the obstacles. Hang in there.

The strongest confidence comes when you know, moment by moment, you are in tune with God.

The strongest confidence comes when you know, moment by moment, you are in tune with God. Jesus is the ultimate source of our endurance, and he lives in you through the person of the Holy Spirit. It is an awesome thing to have the Holy Spirit available to you if you know how to activate his help. But it does you no good to have the resource if you don't have access to it. I loved God for years and unsuccessfully tried to follow his ways, but I didn't understand *how* to walk in the Spirit. It wasn't until someone explained Galatians 5:25 to me that I began to experience God's strength in my daily life: "Since we live by the Spirit, let us keep *in step* with the Spirit" (emphasis added). If I want to carry on a close personal conversation while I am walking with a friend, I must keep in step with my friend. If my friend turns, I must turn also. If there is a fork in the road, we have to take the same road or the conversation will be cut off. The same is true with the Holy Spirit, so my new goal became to stay in step with the Holy Spirit.

Jesus is the ultimate source of our endurance, and he lives in you through the person of the Holy Spirit.

Every season of life requires endurance, and it is only by walking in step with the Spirit that I am able to persevere. He alone gives me the endurance I need to live the life God has called me to. Although I may face many uphill journeys along the way, I know that I will finish the race, walking step by step with the Spirit.

Winning Words

We went through fire and water, but you brought us to a place of abundance. Who has understood the mind of the LORD, or instructed him as his counselor? Whom did the LORD consult to enlighten him, and who taught him the right way? Who was it that taught him knowledge or showed him the path of understanding? To whom, then, will you compare God? What image will you compare him to? Do you not know? Have you not heard? Has it not been told you from the beginning? Have you not understood since the earth was founded? He sits enthroned above the circle of the earth. He stretches out the heavens like a canopy, and spreads them out like a tent to live in. He brings princes to naught and reduces the rulers of this world to nothing. "To whom will you compare me? Or who is my equal?" says the Holy One. Do you not know? Have you not heard? The LORD is the everlasting God, the Creator of the ends of the earth. He will not grow tired or weary, and his understanding no one can fathom. He gives strength to the weary and increases the power of the weak. Even youths grow tired and weary, and young men stumble and fall; but those who hope in the LORD will renew their strength. They will soar on wings like eagles; they will run and not grow weary, they will walk and not be faint.[2]

Winning Ways

Do you feel like you're running out of steam, that you cannot endure any longer? Ask God to lift you up and to give you renewed energy.

Grace Cabalka saw God succeed in part because she lined up her methods with his. God honors order (1 Cor 14:40), so Grace worked hard to get her ducks in a row as much as possible. God calls us to function as a body (1 Cor 12:12), so Grace pulled together a quality team. God says count the costs (Lk 14:28), so Grace weighed out her decision carefully. God also tells us to walk in the Spirit, so Grace asked God for his help at every step.

In a challenge you see as an impossibility in your own life, ask yourself if you are tackling the issue in God's way, in his time and with his team.

15

$\mathcal{P}$ERSPECTIVE

"If Satan can't destroy the dream he will try to destroy the dreamer."
JILL BRISCOE

$\mathcal{W}$hen I first met Monique, I immediately noticed that she was bright, articulate and educated, and I soon learned that she was the co-owner of a business worth about a million dollars. When the topic of church came up, Monique expressed an interest in spiritual things, and she began to attend church. Because she was a woman who wanted the best out of life, she quickly realized that knowing God was the best choice for her and her family so she recommitted her life to Christ. She seemed like a woman who had it all, but I saw a hurt, a pain in her eyes and a woundedness in her spirit that she tried to cover with a bravado of authority and decisiveness.

As Monique grew in her faith, she began to wonder if her priorities were God's best. In her own words, Monique comments on this realization:

I controlled much of the day-to-day operations and administrative and financial responsibilities of the company. The pressure to perform and stay on top was incredible. I asked my husband, "When is enough *enough*?" He had no answer.

I was finally getting the inkling that while I was working toward an end—that of a comfortable living with the opportunity to live in a bigger house, maybe have a few vacations a year, and decide when we were going to retire—my husband's working *was his end*. There was no other definition or aspiration to him. It just had to be the company—bigger and bigger—more and more. There was no goal other than working as hard as he could. He had become just like his own workaholic father.

Because I value achievement, I had been a willing partner in this elusive race for accumulating more and more. I would get up at 5 a.m., work at my kitchen table for two hours, get everyone else up for the day, and go to work about 8 a.m., work until 6 or 7 p.m., come home, go out to dinner with he and the kids, put the kids down for bed and start all over again the next morning. This went on for years! We were building an incredible business but letting the family and marriage go out with the bath water on a daily basis. I knew at some point, it had to stop.

God shuffled the deck of my priorities, and my kids and spiritual life began to take my time and energy. I was finding strength in God, and I was also finding a new freedom from the tyranny of having to always do bigger and better for the company. God was now in control of me rather than the company.[1]

Hindsight

Monique also began to notice that there was an unhealthy pattern at work and at home:

While running the company I was always the one that disciplined, counseled, directed the staff. He was the good guy that everyone could talk to. He would come into my office, shut the door, then go into a rage about something, wanting me to confront and deal with whatever issue it was. I would open the door and "handle" whomever or whatever it was. He maintained his good guy image while I played the bad guy. He and I did this deliberately. At the time I thought it was for the common good, the good of the company and simply the way things worked.

With all that said, I have always been a strong woman. People look at me and think *capable, responsible, don't mess with her.* As I became more in touch with the Lord, I became discontent and uncomfortable with the "bad boss" role. I tried to talk to my husband about it, and he would have nothing to do with changing it, putting what I thought to be God's values on a shelf.

Monique was realizing more and more each day that her entire life was out of perspective. Her marriage had some serious flaws in it as well. She realized that she was being held captive by her husband's compulsive need for sexual gratification.

> When he didn't get the sex he wanted, he would go to work and be in a terrible mood, causing havoc within the company, and only he and I would know why he was in such a mood. It felt like emotional blackmail. It felt like pay up or lose all we've worked for at the company. Give in whenever and wherever, or all I had worked for the kids would vanish before my eyes because of the complications my husband could carry out in the work place. I felt like I was between a rock and a hard place, but I was committed to our marriage, our family and my husband. I wanted the best for us.

At about the same time Monique was questioning things in her life, an old friend reentered the picture:

> Sharon had first come into our lives as a childcare provider that I found through a referral service of the county. She was a licensed day care provider in our area with no blemishes and in good standing. As circumstances changed, the kids went to a Christian childcare, and we lost touch with Sharon. One day, Sharon was selling water door to door and came to our door, not knowing we lived there. We invited her in and talked to her about coming to work in sales for us. I did most of the hiring negotiations and she began. Very shortly thereafter she was having trouble in her marriage. Her husband had slept with her best friend, and she came to me for help and guidance. Over the next year we were very supportive, especially me taking much time from very busy days to help dry her tears and prop her up emotionally and financially. The business flourished through this time with the three of us working so hard.

Monique was hoping that all the hard work would pay off and that her marriage would also flourish. At a marriage conference, Monique decided God wanted her to help her husband by not giving into his irrational control of her and the business because of his sexual desires:

> I made a decision to no longer let his mood affect my moods. I made a paradigm shift. His world was his, and I knew I wasn't the one who could fill the void in his heart and life. That was something only God could do. I felt I needed to keep the world my kids and I dwelt in more healthy, not tossed

around or controlled by one person's negativity and unhealthy behaviors. Interestingly, Sharon was a very close friend by then and she "helped" me to make this paradigm shift. As I think back to it now, I should have known better than to seek her counsel. There were so many things in her life not to respect. I knew she was somewhat "wild." She dressed very provocatively, rarely kept good friends for long periods of time, and she did not have a personal relationship with God.

Monique calmly explained her decision to her husband, and he seemed almost too eager to agree to the change in their relationship. Company business led him out of town more and more, and when he went, Sharon would also go. More and more of their family time became entwined with Sharon and her children. Around Christmas, Monique began to notice even more bizarre behaviors. Her husband didn't want to sleep in their bed, avoided spending time with her and the children and began to have fits of rage that escalated in intensity. Though he never hit her or the children, he did shatter the mirrors in their bedroom.

Monique became alarmed. She asked her husband to go for counseling and to speak to their pastor, but he refused both. Even when their pastor stopped by their home or went to talk to him in the parking lot when picking up their children, her husband refused to communicate. She asked him to open up and share what was going on in his mind, but he still refused. Instead, one day she was served divorce papers. The deception was unmasked. Her husband and Sharon had been having an affair—for a long while.

> To find out that the woman that had cared for my kids, the woman whom I had helped financially and emotionally through her divorce, the woman who was my confidante all the way through the first few months of the divorce process—she was having an affair with my husband. She had been giving him the sex he had told me a year before that he would no longer push me for. He wasn't going to push me because he knew where he was going to find it. And she knew too. I remember asking her way before he even asked me for a divorce. "Do you think he has another woman?" Her response, of course, was "no."
>
> So the betrayal was not just of the marriage bond, it was a betrayal of a close friend and all those people I had given a job to. All the people that

had benefited from my getting up at 5 a.m. and working at my kitchen table . . . ensuring the growth and health of the company. They were all gone, all had turned on me, had abandoned what I thought they believed was important.

Seeing Beyond the Pain

Monique turned to the only source of help and hope she had known in life. She turned to God. "The story here could be one of betrayal and abandonment," says Monique.

> Through Jesus Christ and his shed blood on the cross I know that this story of mine is about hope, faith, renewal of spirit and of the goodness of our Lord and Savior. And it is only the love that he provides and gives to us that is eternal. His love will not betray and will not abandon. He is steadfast when our world is turbulent and when those around us fail and are given to sin and hate.

Even when things went from bad to worse, Monique held on to God and his promises in the Bible. She clung to God's truth and took the high road of integrity even when she received threatening faxes, even when hateful untruths were circulated about her at work, even when sexually explicit messages and notes were left on her voice mail or in her office, even when details of her intimate life were retold in twisted ways to those she was supposed to manage.

Monique took the high road even when her husband drove a forklift through a wall at the company in anger. She took the high road even when the majority of the workers at the company turned against her because of promises of money from her husband. She took the high road when a group of her husband's buddies tried to steal office equipment and the sheriff deputies had to come and draw their weapons. Even when her own company was torn from under her leadership, when her former husband sabotaged accounts and engineered a walkout for three days, costing the company approximately fifty thousand dollars, she still took the high road and clung to truth like a lifeline of hope.

Monique made a conscious choice to allow God to fortify truth into her heart, mind and soul. She decided, not based on feelings, but based on the character of God, that she would walk through these dark days according to his plan and his priorities. She decided to seek to reflect his character, rather than seek revenge or retaliation:

> From early into this divorce I felt power in the situation. The incredible part is that I first felt God's power, and then I saw the strength of Satan. The Lord had fortified me for the battle and was willing to give me the nourishment through it to maintain the fight. To stand up for what is right and just. To turn the other cheek and live this through my own life example. There were times when I wanted to slam my husband, legally and emotionally. Times when that would have been "appropriate" according to the world we live in. Yet I knew that I couldn't do these things the way that had been done to me. What they did was cruel, mean and hateful. I firmly believe that Satan pushed them, as generally people don't continue this stream of hate and cruelty over time . . . and I firmly believe that God sustained me through it all, as I will call on him to do again and again for the rest of my life and for the life of my children.
>
> I have had a spiritual journey of unbelievable depth. It still blows me away to know how good God is to his children. By taking the high road, the road that God calls us to, life is better and his sense of peace and contentment can be yours as a follower of Christ.

Seeing Clearly

Perspective is all about the ability to see clearly, to see the outcome of integrity, and the wisdom and power to step into that integrity. But sometimes, when you seek to be a woman of integrity, the battle goes beyond this small earthly realm, and your life becomes a battleground between God and Satan. As in the life of Job (see Job 1), God often trusts us with a major battle so that others can learn and grow and so that we develop the character or strength we will need for an assignment down the road that we do not yet see. But what steps should we follow in order to maintain perspective when involved in these battles?

Perspective is the ability to see the outcome of integrity before you step into it.

Recognize the enemy. What is the source of the strife in your life? Have you monitored your heart for your motives? Have you checked your life for a wrong turn or a poor choice? Are you tired or ill? If you've ruled out these possibilities, then the enemy in the battle is likely Satan himself. One of Satan's favorite ploys is to turn our thoughts to self-doubt and self-destruction. Neil Anderson, in *The Steps to Freedom in Christ,* asks a small question that captures the essence of a spiritual attack: "Are you having nagging or repeated thoughts contrary to what you think or believe?"[2] Satan is not very creative. He uses the same old lines year after year, person after person, whispering things like, "You're stupid. You'll never get it right. You're ugly. You're worthless. You . . . you . . . you . . ."

Change your perspective. Satan knows he is totally defeated if you shift your perspective off yourself and on to God. James 4:7 says, "Submit yourselves, then, to God. Resist the devil, and he will flee from you." God tells us that he inhabits the praises of his people. It will feel foreign to praise God when things are going wrong, when the world seems upside down, when you are feeling blue about yourself and life in general, but when we don't focus on him, Satan causes us to stumble and become self-absorbed. In my life, Satan's favorite tool to use on me is depression. He tries to rob me of joy and make me feel like a failure. However, I have learned to quickly recognize his work, and I ask myself, "What's the truth here?" I have a ready list of "winning words" about victory through Christ and the power of God that quickly refocuses my heart and helps me gain perspective.

Rally the troops. You need trusted friends to point out the truth in your life and point you back to God. A strong woman has several trusted confidants, who she can be real with. In our ministry we encourage women to have at least a handful of honest and straightforward women in her life, who will point her back to God. Debe is one of those women in my life. She was the first woman I trained for ministry when I came to the church I currently serve over twelve years ago. A talented writer and the music/drama director of our church, she is a woman who understands the power of praise and proclaiming God's Word to clarify life and regain strength.

Once I was struggling with self-doubt, and I didn't have any one thing to pin it on. I was feeling like a failure even though I had just experienced some of my life's greatest successes months before. I had some successful books, I was enjoying traveling for speaking and media, I had a great marriage, my three sons were all doing well, and our women's ministry had just finished a big event that had an incredible impact in our community. But I had put on some weight in my traveling, I was dead-dog tired, and I needed a vacation. Then someone said something extremely insensitive and hurtful to me.

Normally, I am very optimistic, but even the rational logical evidence for positive success in my life was being clouded over and crowded out by this growing sense of impending failure. Mountains were being made from molehills on every front of my mind. Usually I'd be able to take those things in stride, make changes and go forward, but severe negative thoughts were plaguing me daily, so I called Debe to pray with me. I shared with Debe what was going on in my life, and as Debe prayed for me, God gave her a visual impression in her mind of what I was going through. She said to me:

> Pam, I saw you looking into a puddle of water at your reflection. The water was so clear you could see yourself in this liquid mirror. Suddenly, someone threw a rock into the puddle. The water became rippled, and the reflection was distorted. Pam, the rock represents the person who has criticized you and hurt you, and the rippled water is how you are seeing yourself as a result. The real Pam, the one God sees, is the same as you saw in the water's reflection before the rock was thrown into the puddle . The real Pam is unharmed—*only your image has been affected* by the rock—not the real you!

Give your life away. Perspective comes when you bear one anther's burdens (Gal 6:2). One of the best ways to regain perspective is to get your eyes off yourself. In those tough times when the rocks of criticism and hate splash in, the best way to calm the waters so you can see a clear reflection is to step out of your small mindset and step into God's.

Once when I was feeling that life was not worth living, I began to entertain thoughts of escaping and running away, which escalated into thoughts of a final escape—death. The fact that I even entertained the thought shakes me to my core, but my mentor Jill Briscoe says, "If Satan can't destroy the dream, he will try to destroy the dreamer."

Fortunately, God had layered some good training so I could take those thoughts captive. At the same time, I got a call informing me of the impending death of a friend, so I went to visit her. The hospice worker was there, signs of terminal illness everywhere, and the faces of the family reflected that death was on their doorstep. As I went to the side of my dying friend, I saw the full impact, the truth of what death really is: *hard, painful, final.* That day, my friend, in a coma, saved my life because my eyes shifted focus and saw life as it really was, no distortions, just the facts—my friend needed me, right then, and her family needed me more. I had to pull myself together because the days ahead would be rough for this family, and I knew I was called to help carry them through these rough waters. God, whom I had been blaming and pushing away because of my depression, suddenly became my best friend again as I confessed my self-centered attitude and thanked him for his patience, love, grace and power.

Seeing the Fruit

When Monique found herself engaged in the biggest battle of her life, she was comforted by God's Word and noted the verses in a journal so she could refer back to them on tough days. Monique recorded God's faithfulness to her and her children. The most powerful of Monique's journal entries is one where she weighs out a recurring dream she is having during the horrendous divorce proceedings. "I'd been having a recurring dream about flying. Early on the Lord began to speak to me, and I believe he chose this dream to communicate that when we have our eyes *beyond* ourselves, he will take us to an even higher place." The entry reads:

> As I was dreaming, it dawned on me that when I concentrate on a point at which to go, that is in my viewpoint, it is hard to get off the ground in order to fly. It is when I gaze at the horizon, to a point that I have no clear vision of, further than I can see and focus on; I am lifted immediately and go flying without hindrance. . . . I am to set my sights beyond what I see or know. God will take me beyond and it should not be a fearful time but a time that helps me to know that God has set the point of destination and he will protect and lift me to the place he has planned for me.

Monique couldn't see the future God had planned for her, but she kept stepping out in integrity. She and her support group prayed for God's perspective and power before the myriad of court appearances for both custody hearings and property and business hearings, "Lord, let the truth be brought to light. Shed your light of truth in the courtroom today."

In the end, though the running of the business was taken out of her hands, the court awarded her a full salary and benefits as if she worked for her company, allowing her to be a full-time mom, to spend much time helping her children though the transition, building their faith and volunteering at their school. She was given a fair settlement from the business that paid for her return to college for a higher degree and a new home for her children. And because she maintained her integrity and grew so much in her relationship with God, a large church in the area has hired her in ministry.

When you gain God's perspective, he gives you the ability to hear the applause from heaven.

Today Monique feels like a winner. It isn't the money that makes her feel that way, although it does provide for Monique and her children, nor is it the fact that her husband is now sorry he ever got involved with another woman and he is reaping some heavy consequences for his rebellion against God and his standards. More than anything, what makes Monique feel like a winner is that she came out of a whirlwind with her integrity intact when she could have been destroyed from the inside out. By the grace of God, she was given a heavenly perspective, a perspective that only comes when we focus on him and tune our lives to his heart. And when you gain God's perspective, he also gives you the ability to hear the applause from heaven—there's nothing like it.

Winning Words
Do not take revenge, my friends, but leave room for God's wrath, for it is written: "It is mine to avenge; I will repay," says the LORD. On the contrary: "If your enemy is hungry, feed him; if he is thirsty, give him something to drink. In doing this, you will heap burning coals on his head." Do not be overcome by evil, but overcome evil with good.

He ransoms me unharmed from the battle waged against me, even though many oppose me. O Sovereign LORD, my strong deliverer, who shields my head in the day of battle— The horse is made ready for the day of battle, but victory rests with the LORD. All those gathered here will know that it is not by sword or spear that the LORD saves; for the battle is the LORD's, and he will give all of you into our hands. This is what the LORD says to you: "Do not be afraid or discouraged because of this vast army. For the battle is not yours, but God's." In your unfailing love, silence my enemies; destroy all my foes, for I am your servant. He will swallow up death in victory; and the LORD God will wipe away tears from off all faces; and the rebuke of his people shall he take away from off all the earth: for the LORD hath spoken it. Sing to the LORD a new song, for he has done marvelous things; his right hand and his holy arm have worked salvation for him. But thanks be to God! He gives us the victory through our Lord Jesus Christ . . . for everyone born of God overcomes the world. This is the victory that has overcome the world, even our faith.[3]

Winning Ways

Is there someone in your life who has hurt you, held you back, betrayed you? In Proverbs 23:7 (KJV) it says, "For as he thinketh in his heart, so is he," meaning that if all you keep thinking about is the person that has done you wrong—you will become like that person! It's natural for us to want revenge, but God asks us to place the situation in his hands. Only by handing the battle over to the Lord will you be free to go forward in life. If you keep mulling that injustice, betrayal and hurt over in your mind, you are handing over control of your life to the very person who hurt you!

Ask God to give you perspective in those tight places. Ask him for wisdom and clarity. Give control of your life back over to God and allow him to fight the battle for you today. Gain perspective by focusing on a positive goal in the distance and do *something* today to take a step toward it.

16

$\mathcal{T}$ENACITY

"Far away, there in the sunshine, are my highest aspirations.
I may not reach them but I can look up and see their beauty,
believe in them, and try to follow where they lead."
LOUISA MAY ALCOTT

$\mathcal{T}$he Torch Center towers above Seoul, Korea, sixty stories high, shaped like praying hands, home to numerous ministries and businesses, including the Korean Center for World Mission. Since the center's completion in 1991, it has become the training center for missions for a multitude of denominations across Korea. Sixty students each year receive their doctorate in missions under scholarships sponsored by the center, and in 1995, 186 nations met at the Torch Center for Global Congress on World Evangelism. The tower is a beacon of hope to all Korea and a monument to the faith of a tiny Korean woman named Lee Hyung-Ja.

How could a tiny woman in Asia facilitate such a dramatic tower of faith and business, especially considering she was on the brink of bankruptcy just years before? The secret might be found in the basement of the Torch Center where shoes line the walls outside the prayer room. Here, prayers are offered daily in the dozens of prayer cells that run like arteries to the heart—the heart of the Korean Center for World Mission and the heart of Lee's businesses.

Life was not always rosy for Lee. Her husband, Choi Soon-Young, had inherited the family baking business with over a million dollars in debt, and they had another family business that was draining their funds. Bankruptcy seemed inevitable. Lee was worried about her husband's health and worried about her family's future, so she garnished her strength, and in a culture where appearances and outward success are highly valued, she bowed before the bank president. The president refused her request.

Lee looked at her heart. Had she really been trusting God? Convicted, she began to rise at 4 a.m. daily to pray. As she prayed she gained confidence that God had her life and her husband's business in his hands. Soon she began to have specific answers and ideas for her husband's business. When she'd share them with her husband, he could immediately see the wisdom of these ideas. The two began to pray together every morning at 4 a.m., and her husband began to rely on his wife's guidances from God, calling her from work to pray over specific decisions during the day. The business began to revive, and their new construction company was building equity daily. Lee and her husband felt amazingly blessed, as the country of Korea was experiencing political unrest and economic downturn during this time.

Lee and her husband looked at the huge profits and decided the amount was too much just to give to one institution, so they decided to help growing churches and loaned a church money for construction. One morning shortly after the business began to grow, Lee was impressed by the Holy Spirit to "light every dry branch, and pass the torches from mountain peak to mountain peak. Raise the torch of the Holy Spirit high above and pass it unto the end of the world." So Lee gathered a group of four women to pray in her living room. Week after week they prayed for God's leading, their country, their families, churches and revival. Word about the prayer meetings spread, and others joined in. Soon, groups were springing up across the nation, and the decision was made to form a regular prayer meeting called "The Torch Assembly."

In 1977, The Torch Assembly, for the purpose of better organizing its meetings, registered with the Ministry of Culture and Publicity as a nonprofit religious organization under its current name, "The Korean Center for World Mission." In the years to follow, the idea came to build the magnificent Torch Center. And it all started with one woman's tenacious prayers and her belief that God's unlimited power would carry them through.

Picturing God in Your Future

Tenacity is the ability to hold on to God and allow him to carry you through. When everything around you feels like it's falling apart and you're not sure if you can handle the fears and the doubts, tenacity is calling out to God, offering up prayer after prayer, asking for his power. And he gives it. Like Peter, who walked on water in the middle of the storm, we can keep walking as long as we keep our eyes on God. The minute we rely on our own strength to see us through, however, we begin to sink.

When everything around you feels like it's falling apart and you're not sure if you can handle the fears and the doubts, tenacity is calling out to God, offering up prayer after prayer, asking for his power.

Char Hill feels like an ordinary woman, but I know from experience that her tenacious attitude towards life is anything from ordinary. I was introduced to Char by my sister-in-law Erin. Erin, a wonderful godly woman herself, would always tell me she wished she could have the strength and femininity of Char, a woman who could pour cement for a missions project in a foreign country one day, then quilt and can garden vegetables the next, who could build an entire home herself, but also loved to nurture and mother. Erin told me that Char, who owned her own café, once held two robbers at gunpoint until the police came. And while setting up an interview for me with Char, Erin mentioned that Char had recently roofed a house.

I began to see Char as some kind of modern day pioneer women, a Paul Bunyan of sorts, a woman of whom legends and tall tales are made! When I finally met Char, however, her calm, quiet, "can do" attitude was a breath of fresh air, and I began to understand where her strength comes from.

"Everyone thinks I am so strong, but they don't know my mother! I'm just a shadow of my mother," explains Char.

> The things I do are normal to me. My mother was widowed three times. She had four kids when her husband had a heart attack. Pouring concrete, tearing out a tree, raising animals—this is what you had to do. If it needs done,

you do it. God will take care of you, but he expects you to take care of yourself too. My mother knew God would take care of her, give her the strength, no matter what, so it's natural for me to depend on God for everything.

Char grew up knowing she could achieve anything with God's help and that eternal values mattered more than pretty things or an easy life.

Char relied on the power of God to sustain her during a particularly challenging time of life:

> I had an unwanted divorce and cancer at the same time. I had two kids, both in junior high. I was alone, and I had never been alone (I married at 17). I had to let God be the man in my life. I saw my main role was to keep their lives together. God really got my attention. Physical things were not important. Who got what in the divorce was not important. I just wanted to live to raise my kids.

Char's hair grew thin. She lost weight and had blisters in her mouth and throat so she couldn't keep food down. Things looked grim.

> I hadn't told my family I had cancer. Not wanting them to worry, I explained that I was real sick and was working hard. One day, I was sitting in the back of the church, and in the middle of the sermon, the pastor stopped and said, "God wants me to pray, pray for someone whose whole world is falling apart." Up to that point, I thought God had forgotten me, I had prayed and prayed and thought angry things like, "God, I've served you my whole life, and I am falling apart!"

Shortly after that day in church the nurses rechecked Char's white blood cell count.

> Over and over they checked and ran tests—no cancer! It was not showing up in any of the blood work or anything. I knew then I had better stay close to God. I had better not ever get one step away from being in his will. I told God, "If you think you want me to married again, if another man is your will—*you* pick him out!"

Then in typical Char fashion, while helping friends move, Char met her current husband. "He is the best thing that ever happened to me. And the doctors said I'd never have kids—but less than a year later I was pregnant with Sarah."

"Looking back at disastrous things, you see they made you stronger, and I believe those things made my kids stronger. They've learned they need to give it to God, and he'll handle it." Char had learned that life is hard, but she had also learned that the verse her mother had always quoted was true as well: *All things are possible with God.*

Picturing God

When we go through rough times in life, God doesn't stand idly by. He is willing, ready and able to intercede to accomplish his will, his perfect will. He has the power to win over anything, anyone, at anytime. At times it may seem that he has abandoned us, but we can't see all the pieces of God's puzzle. We lack information, perspective and most of all, patience. But when we go to his Word and study his character, we find that God has carefully woven many pictures of himself into the text so we can gain a better view of who he is and how he works.

He will protect me in times of battle, and I can run to him to gain perspective on the people and things attacking my life.

One summer I discovered many of these word pictures when I was teaching my sons about how the Bible came to us. As we followed the Bible from its initial writing to the modern text we have today, we studied the different time periods throughout history. One day, I decided to give the boys a real medieval experience by making them each a suit of armor, a milk carton helmet, swords and shields. When we got to the shields, I wondered how big to make them, so I pulled out books. But then I wondered what shields were like in Bible times. As I did the research, I realized that my view of a shield was based more on images from Disney than on the truth from God's word.

During biblical times, shields were three-sided, as tall as a man and covered with leather and metal. Learning this, I gained a fuller understanding of what the psalmist meant when he said that God was my shield. I was comforted by the fact that the only way to get hurt in battle was to step out from behind the shield—or run in retreat. I also realized that because God is my shield, everything that comes to me in life must first go through him.

Intrigued, I wondered what other word pictures there were in the Psalms that could give me insight on God's character, so I looked up all the verses that had to do with defensive weapons in the Psalms. I discovered that God was my rock, a high place upon which a fortified city is built. I also read he was my fortress, a walled-in city. God said he was a rampart, an elevated rise on which walls of shelter were erected in times of battle. Then I read that he was my bulwark, which is a round tower that sits at each corner of the fortress where the soldiers would run to gain perspective on attacking enemies.

Now those are some word pictures I can depend on! God wants to be my high place of refuge, a place in which I can run and be safe and still have my basic needs met. He will protect me in times of battle, and I can run to him to gain perspective on the people and things attacking my life.

Choosing to Follow the Lord

When I am tempted to give up in an area of life, to throw in the towel or pull up short, I review the character of God and the names of God, like those revealed in the Old Testament. My favorite name of God is *Jehovah Jireh*, meaning "the one who provides." When things get tough, this name reminds me that God is my provision, and I need to choose to please him first. During really intense times, I review a few principles:

☐ I will make my choices based upon what will guard my integrity before God, regardless of popular opinion.

☐ I will ask God to go before me, to pave the way on my behalf.

☐ I will see if God is leading me to readjust my timing or my plan.

☐ I will regroup, readjust and redelegate.

☐ I will rely on God's strength. I remind myself that God doesn't set me up for failure. My failures are just footsteps into the future God has for me.

I also call to mind 2 Corinthians 4:8-9: "We are hard pressed on every side, but not crushed; perplexed, but not in despair; persecuted, but not abandoned; struck down, but not destroyed." *Pressed in* means "in a vice"—the walls are closing in. But God says we *won't* be crushed. God stands between me and the tsunami of responsibility threatening my world. Instead of worrying, instead of fuming, instead of taking my feelings out on someone else, I review God's amazing traits, sometimes out loud—because I need to hear them! God is awesome, beautiful, caring and compassionate . . .

God stands between me and the tsunami of responsibility threatening my world.

God's power is unlimited, ever available, unwavering, steadfast, sure and tenacious. Women who have this view of God can achieve much more than those who believe in only their own power. Self-power is limited, fragile or can be misdirected, but if we ask, God will answer, and he will send his ultimate best our way. He will provide you with the tenacity you need to achieve the dreams he has given you.

Winning Words
I call on you, O God, for you will answer me; give ear to me and hear my prayer. Hear my voice when I call, O LORD; be merciful to me and answer me. I will call upon you in the day of trouble; you will deliver me, and will honor me. But I call to God, and the LORD saves me. Then my enemies will turn back when I call for help. By this I will know that God is for me. If God is for me, who can be against me? From the ends of the earth I call to you, I call as my heart grows faint; lead me to the rock that is higher than I. You are forgiving and good, O LORD, abounding in love to all who call to you. Lord, you say, "He will call upon me, and I will answer him; I will be with him in trouble, I will deliver him and honor him." I call out to you; save me and I will keep your statutes. I call on the LORD in my distress, and he answers me. The LORD is near to all who call on him, to all who call on him in truth.[1]

Winning Ways
Do you have a plan to handle bad days? If I have a series of strenuous, unpleasant days ahead, I begin with prayer and ask God to pull me through those rough days. I also reward for myself for getting through tough times with favorite tasks like calling a friend or going to the beach. Knowing there's a light at the end of the tunnel gives me the tenacity to pull through and keeps me from spiraling down into a long-term depression.

Create your own crisis plan for handling the blues—one that builds into your life and helps you deepen your walk with God.

☐ Build mental pictures of God into your mind by purchasing a musical CD or cassette that highlights praise music, words of Scripture set to music.

☐ When you are having one of those days, close your eyes, put on your headset and let his presence wash over you.

☐ Buy a piece of art for your office or bedroom that helps you remember your favorite attribute of God.

☐ Create a piece of art, screensaver, craft, etc., to help you picture God as your strength on those bluest of days.

☐ Create your own retreat: a quiet corner of the office, a special chair with a basket of books, a fountain, waterfall in your yard or on the patio, someplace you can go open up the Psalms and gain a clear glimpse of God.

☐ Place something small in your wallet, checkbook or briefcase that will remind you of an attribute of God that gives you strength, perhaps a small stone to remind you that God is your rock.

☐ If you have many "blue days" strung together, professional help may be the best plan. In every other arena of life when women of confidence need answers, they go to the best in whatever field they need answers in—handling depression should be the same. Investing in your emotional health is a wise investment of God's resources in you.

Appendix

$\mathscr{A}$CCOUNTABILITY

$\mathscr{A}$ woman of confidence needs to have an accountability partner—someone she can trust to be honest with her about her strengths and her weaknesses, someone who will encourage in the hard times and rejoice in the good. I like to think of an accountability partner as a fine-tuning friend, like the electric tuner my husband uses to tune his guitar. He can judge pretty well by ear if the guitar is in tune, but the electric tuner makes it even more precise. The same is true of a woman who has a few good fine-tuning friends.

Accountability isn't really a biblical term, but the principle of accountability is found in the Bible where we read the word *exhortation,* a term that means "called alongside to bring out the best in another." *Exhortation* is made up of two Greek words: παρα which means "alongside" and κλε̄σις which means "calling." It carries the idea of compassionate encouragement to do your best. *Admonish* is another biblical term that describes the principle of accountability: It literally means "to put in mind" and carries the idea of putting the right thoughts into the minds of others.

A few well-chosen fine-tuning friends can become a great source of strength for you, but it really only works if you want it to! The condition of your heart is vital to the success of an accountability relationship. A tender, contrite, repentant heart that wants God's best and God's growth is fertile ground. A ready heart is the instrument God needs in order to use your fine-tuning friend to tune you to his will for your life.

Finding a Fine-Tuning Friend

When you look for a fine-tuning friend, here a few questions to consider.

☐ Is she a natural friend that you'd like to spend more time with?

☐ Is she part of your world enough to see your marriage, your interactions with children, coworkers, volunteers, etc.?

☐ Can this woman keep confidences?

☐ Does she have credibility in your eyes?

☐ Has she been through the fire of life? Do you respect her?

☐ Does she know Jesus as well or better than you?

☐ Will she be a prayer advocate who will consistently lift you, your life and your concerns to the Father in heaven?

I have found these traits most helpful in helping hone me. For example, I need a friend who knows Christ at about my level so that as I struggle through life issues, I know she will send me to Scriptures that will get my attention. I need her to be a woman who has gone through trials in her life so that she can relate to me when I hit my own. As I see *how* a woman goes through tough times, I gain respect and confidence that she will have something to say when I hit my own bumps in the road. However, the two traits most imperative to me are her abilities to keep a confidence and her desire to pray for me consistently. I have come to believe that prayer is how any forward movement in life is won, and I need a friend whom I can honestly share specifics with so we can commit them to prayer and trust God to give his answers in his way at his time.

One of the most important first prayers of a woman of confidence who desires to achieve with integrity is, "Lord, send me a fine-tuning friend!"

Questions to Help You Fine-Tune Each Other

At one retreat I attended, each woman was encouraged to get and keep accountability partners. Below are questions from a bookmark that was handed to each woman to carry in her Bible. Use these questions when talking with your fine-tuning friend about your lives.

1. Have talked to someone about Jesus this week?

2. Have you managed your time wisely?

3. Have you taken time to thank the Lord this week? Have you had your quiet times?

4. Have you had a good attitude toward your spouse and children this week?

5. Have you said damaging things about another person either behind their back or to their face?

6. Have you succumbed to a personal addiction?

7. Have you continued to remain angry toward another?

8. Have you fantasized a romantic relationship with someone other than your spouse, or read or seen any sexually alluring material?

9. Have you lacked integrity in your financial dealings? Have you spent recklessly?

10. Have you secretly wished for another's misfortune so that you might excel?

11. Have you been completely truthful with me just now?

The next year at the same retreat, I got to see and hear the results of the women who made the step of finding accountability partners and asking these questions on a regular basis. Many came to personal faith, affairs were ended, parenting skills and confidence in mothering increased, businesses started running according to God's principles, addictive behaviors ceased, etc. There was an excitement in the room as women shared, and I believe they were excited because they had a clear conscience, knowing they had achieved with integrity.

When You Are the Tuner

Confronting in love is never easy, but I use this simple exercise to better prepare me when I feel God is asking me to confront a friend.

Know. Write down the facts, what you know intellectually about an issue. For example, you might write: "I know you slammed the door, yelled and then threw down your briefcase." Do not try to guess why! This is more like a scientific observation; just write down the facts—not any interpretation of actions or reactions.

The most important observation is that of my own feelings, motives and stresses over the friend or issue. First and foremost, I ask myself, "Is this even my issue?" Have I earned the right to speak into her life? Am I the best person to do this? Am I doing this because of an unmet emotional need in my own life? My rule is, "If in doubt, don't confront." However, if I am sensing my concern and care is exactly what God wants, I pray through my own fears till I reach obedience. I wait for God's green light.

Feel. How do you feel emotionally about this issue? How do you think she is feeling? I try to walk a mile in her pumps. By looking at life through her eyes, I usually get a sense of whether I need to encourage, confront or remain silent and pray. God usually gives me a sense of timing of what I should or shouldn't say and when I should or shouldn't say it.

Do. What are some options? Brainstorm and make a "problems to solve" list. I also create a "questions to ask" list. I don't want to go in accusing, rather trying to gain information for greater understanding. I try to come up with as many positive options as I can to see if there might be a win-win solution or a way to present the issue and allow my friend to come to her own godly conclusions herself.

When it comes time to meet with my friend, I review what God's Word says about confronting a believer in Matthew 18:15-17:

> If your brother sins against you, go and show him his fault, just between the two of you. If he listens to you, you have won your brother over. But if he will not listen, take one or two others along, so that "every matter may be established by the testimony of two or three witnesses." If he refuses to listen to them, tell it to the church; and if he refuses to listen even to the church, treat him as you would a pagan or a tax collector.

Then, I follow the steps that Jesus told to his disciples.

1. Go privately. If your message is received well, you've won a friend.

2. If meeting #1 didn't go well, go with another who is credible and close to the friend.

3. If step two doesn't achieve the result of bringing your friend back to God, bring the issue to a small group of believers who are willing to walk alongside the friend if she does repent and return to Christ. Choose these friends with the same standards as you would a fine-tuning friend.

4. If the friend still does not repent, treat her as someone who does not know Jesus and show her his love by telling her all about him!

When You Are Being Tuned Up
Sometimes being tuned up is even harder than tuning others. When you are confronted by one of your fine-tuning friends, try to follow these guidelines for receiving their message.

☐ Receive it with grace no matter how it is given.

☐ Don't take it personally no matter how personal the attack.

☐ Consider the source. My fine-tuning friend has a greater hearing in my heart than an unsigned letter or a person with gapping blind spots of integrity in her own life.

☐ Take it to the Father in heaven; pray about it.

☐ If it is a lie, take it captive and refuse to receive it emotionally.

☐ If it is from God, God has usually already brought it up already in other times, places or through his Word. Ask him to let you know how to proceed with this new information and to heal any hurts emotionally.

When I think of my fine-tuning friends, I recall a story of one of the Bible's great leaders, Moses. God asked him to hold his arms up in praise for the duration of a battle and in doing so, Israel would gain God's favor and victory would be assured:

> So Joshua fought the Amalekites as Moses had ordered, and Moses, Aaron and Hur went to the top of the hill. As long as Moses held up his hands, the Israelites were winning, but whenever he lowered his hands, the Amalekites were winning. When Moses' hands grew tired, they took a stone and put it under him and he sat on it. Aaron and Hur held his hands

up—one on one side, one on the other—so that his hands remained steady till sunset. (Ex 17:10-12)

As a woman who desires achievement, you need trusted friends who can hold you up as the battle of life carries on. My fine-tuning friends have held me up in prayer, honest words and with action.

Recently my best friend, the one who can read the stress on my face and even in my voice over the phone, sent me a copy of the same e-mail I had sent her three years ago after my father died. It was an e-mail that listed four areas of life I needed (and still need) her to hold me accountable for. But it was also a thank you. Here are a few of the opening lines:

> Thanks for being such a good friend. I have been reflecting lately, and I think that you are the closest thing to a best friend I have ever had. I just don't let myself be totally open and real with many people. But I am learning to be with you because you ask me. You pick up on things. You are so clued into my pain because we had some kindred experiences growing up and similar things trigger us. Anyway, I wanted to thank you for something very small and natural on your part that meant much to me. . . . Even though you didn't know it, I needed that expression of closer friendship (I didn't even know it until it was given). Thanks for being willing to be patient as I learn to be more candid.

My friend and I have encouraged one another through all kinds of seasons in our own lives, including issues with both of our children, the deaths of family members, health issues and personal issues. We have celebrated my first book and celebrated again many years later when another hit the bestseller list. We have rejoiced over our children's and husbands' triumphs. We have rejoiced even more over personal triumphs in battles we had seen won in prayer that almost no one else even knew about. Because we have committed ourselves to being women who make a difference in this world, we are kindred spirits intent to keep our integrity since we see it as a conduit of influence. However, it is our relationship of honesty that keeps us moving forward in confidence.

She has prayed me through many a book and many a speaking engagement. She is now praying for me as I tackle the "battle of the bulge." I have encouraged her as she has faced down her own set of fears and stepped into the confidence God had waiting for her, like a parent holding a comfortable coat. God holds out to each of us our own coat of many colors. Just as Joseph's father held out that beautiful multicolored coat to his treasured son as a way to honor him, so God has a coat of confidence for you (Gen 37:3; Gal 3:27). To me, my fine-tuning friend is like the coat-check attendant at the finest of restaurants: She has my number! But she is also ready and willing to get my coat and help me put it on so I can go through the front door and out into the world to achieve with integrity.

Notes

Chapter 1: Confidence

[1]Andrea Cooper, "Think You've got Stress?" *Ladies Home Journal,* February 2001, p. 71.

[2]Clayton E. Tucker-Ladd, "Methods for Changing Our Thoughts, Attitudes, Self-Concept, Motivation, Values, and Expectations," in *Psychological Self-Help* (1995-2000) <http://mentalhelp.net/psyhelp/chap14/chap14b.html>.

[3]Holly Firfer, "Study indicates doctors need training to spot depression," CNN.com (January 11, 2000) <www.cnn.com/2000/HEALTH/01/11/managed.care.depression/index.html >.

[4]"The Psychology of Bad Hair Days," CNN.com (January 26, 2000) <www.cnn.com/2000/STYLE/fashion/01/26/bad.hair.ap/index.html>.

[5]Julia Ponder, "7 Habits of Confident Women," *Moneyminded,* March 23, 2000 <www.moneyminded.com/wprklife/ahead/03rb7h11.htm.p.2 >.

[6]A. W. Tozer, *Knowledge of the Holy* (New York: HarperCollins, 1961), p. 1.

[7]Henry Blackaby and Claude King, *Experiencing God* (Nashville: Lifeway, 1990), p. 109.

[8]J. B. Phillips, *Your God is Too Small* (New York: Collier, 1961), p. 42.

[9]Anne Graham Lotz, ed., *Daily Light on the Daily Path* (Nashville: J. Countryman, 1998), March 8 evening reading. Verses: 2 Timothy 1:12; Ephesians 3:20; 2 Corinthians 9:8; Hebrews 2:18; 7:25; Jude 24; 2 Timothy 1:12; Philippians 3:21; Matthew 9:28-29.

[10]Psalm 71:5; Proverbs 3:25-26 paraphrased; Ephesians 3:12 paraphrased; Philippians 1:6 paraphrased; Hebrews 4:16 paraphrased; 1 John 5:14-15 paraphrased; Hebrews 6:9 paraphrased; 10:19-23 paraphrased.

Chapter 2: Opportunity

[1]Heather's story and quotes can be found in her book *Listening with My Heart* (New York: Doubleday, 1997).

[2]Thomas Edison, in *Quotez* (May 28, 2001) <www.digiserve.co.uk/quotations/search.cgi>.

[3]Chuck Swindoll, *Two Steps Forward, Three Steps Back* (Nashville: Thomas Nelson, 1980), p. 74.

[4]Ephesians 3:20 paraphrased; Job 37:23 paraphrased; Isaiah 40:10 paraphrased; 40:29 paraphrased; Jeremiah 32:17 paraphrased; Daniel 6:27 paraphrased; Romans 15:13.

Chapter 3: Priorities

[1]Shirley Weber, speech given at 100 Women in White Conference, San Diego, Calif., October 5, 1997.

[2]Oseola's story and quotes can be found in her book *Simple Wisdom* (Atlanta: Longstreet, 1996).

[3]Ecclesiastes 3:11 paraphrased; Revelation 21:6; Isaiah 55:9; Philippians 2:3-5; Ephesians 1:4; 1 Peter 1:16.

Chapter 4: Failure

[1]Ramona Cramer Tucker, "Enough Is Enough," *Today's Christian Woman*, September-October 1996, p. 128.

[2]Psalm 41:4; 2 Samuel 24:14 paraphrased; Nehemiah 9:31 paraphrased; 13:22; Job 9:15; Psalm 31:22; 40:11; 51:1; 57:1; 79:8 paraphrased; 86:3; 119:132; 123:3 paraphrased; 1 Kings 8:50 paraphrased; Psalms 143:1; Micah 7:18; Luke 1:50 paraphrased; James 3:17; Hebrews 4:16; 1 Peter 1:3; James 2:13.

Chapter 5: Risk

[1]Stephanie Edwards shared her story with me in a personal interview on April 26, 2000.

[2]When I interviewed Debra Maffit on April 28, 2000, she shared her story with me.

[3]I interviewed Holly McClure on April 26, 2000, and she told me her story.

[4]Ephesians 3:20; Philippians 1:6; 1 Corinthians 1:9; James 1:17; Psalm 27:11; 31:3; 143:10; Proverbs 4:11; Isaiah 42:16 paraphrased; 30:21.

Chapter 6: Clarity

[1]Charles Dudley Warner, "The Story of Uncle Tom's Cabin," *Atlantic Monthly* 78 (1896): 311-21.

[2]Attributed to Harriet Beecher Stowe (accessed June 20, 2001) <www.bemorecreative.com/-one/298.html>.

[3]W. Bingham Hunter, *The God Who Hears* (Downers Grove, Ill.: InterVarsity Press, 1986), p. 18.

[4]Ibid., pp. 20, 26.

[5]Ibid., p. 23.

[6]Bill Bright, *God: Discover His Character* (Orlando, Fla.: New Life, 1999), p. 131.

[7]Nathan Stone, *The Names of God* (Chicago: Moody Press, 1944), pp. 97, 99.

[8]Bright, *God: Discover His Character*, p. 131.

[9]Hunter, *The God Who Hears*, p. 20.

[10]Psalm 37:28; 99:4; Exodus 23:2, 6; Leviticus 19:15; Deuteronomy 16:19-20; Psalm 37:6; 106:3; 112:5; Proverbs 21:15; 28:5; 29:7; Isaiah 1:17; Jeremiah 9:24; Hosea 12:6; Amos 5:24.

Chapter 7: Potential

[1]Sojourner Truth, speech at the 1851 Women's Rights Convention in Akron, Ohio, <www.sojournertruth.org/Library/Speeches/AintIAWoman.htm>.

[2]Harriet Beecher Stowe, *Sojourner Truth, The Libyan Sibyl,* posted on AFRO-American Almanac <www.toptags.com/aama/books/book6.html>.

[3]Ibid.

[4]Ibid.

[5]Ibid.

[6]*Strong's Greek and Hebrew Dictionary,* #5011, Wordsearch software (Colorado Springs: NavPress, 1987).

[7]Ibid., #7812.

[8]Isaiah 6:1-8.

Chapter 8: Networking

[1]Mary Crowley's story and quotes can be found in her book *You Can Too* (Grand Rapids, Mich.: Baker, 1976).

[2]Mary Kay's story and quotes can be found in her book *Mary Kay* (New York: Harper Col-

lins, 1994).

[3]Psalm 6:4; 17:7; 18:1; 21:7; 26:3; 31:16; 32:10; 33:18, 22; 36:10; 44:26; 57:10; 59:16; 94:18; 119:76; 143:8.

[4]Crowley, *You Can Too*, p. 36.

[5]Ibid., p. 56.

Chapter 9: Peace

[1]Charles Price at Forest Home, "Living in a Situation," August 1999, audiotape.

[2]Numbers 6:26; 1 Kings 2:33; Psalm 29:11; Micah 5:4-5; John 14:27; 16:33; Romans 5:1-2; 1 Corinthians 14:33; Ephesians 2:14; Philippians 4:7; Colossians 3:15; 2 Thessalonians 3:16.

[3]*Easton's 1897 Bible Dictionary*, WordSearch software (Colorado Springs: NavPress, 1987). "It denotes the true humanity of our Lord. He had a true body (Hebrews 2:14; Luke 24:39) and a rational soul. He was perfect man."

Chapter 10: Vision

[1]JoeAnn Ballard shared her story with me in a personal interview on August 18, 1998.

[2]*Worldwide Challenge*, December 1981, p. 20.

[3]Earl Roe, *Dream Big* (Ventura, Calif.: Gospel Light, 1990), p. 57.

[4]2 Samuel 22:29; Psalm 19:8; 36:9; 43:3; 119:105; Ephesians 5:14.

Chapter 11: Focus

[1]Helen's story and quotes can be found in her book *The Story Goes On* (Kansas City, Mo.: Stonecroft Ministries, 1984).

[2]Dallas Willard, *Hearing God* (Downers Grove, Ill.: InterVarsity Press, 1999), p. 71.

[3]Ibid., p. 90.

[4]Ibid., pp. 84-85.

[5]Luke 7:50; John 10:9; Acts 2:21; 4:12; 15:11; 16:31; Romans 5:9-10; 10:9-10, 13; Psalm 69:13.

Chapter 12: Courage

[1]Flo-Jo's story and quotes come from Phil Newman, "Go with the Flo-Jo," *Aspire*, June-July 1996, pp. 24-25.

[2]Joshua 1:9; Deuteronomy 31:8; Ezra 10:4; Joshua 1:7; Psalm 31:2; 61:3; 140:7; Proverbs 18:10; 23:11; Ephesians 6:10-11; 1 Peter 5:10; 1 John 2:14; Romans 8:37.

Chapter 13: Creativity

[1]LeeAnn shared her story with me in a personal interview in April 2000.

[2]Henry M. Morris, "Impact103: Bible-Believing Scientists of the Past," Institute for Creation Research, PO Box 2667, El Cajon, CA 92021.

[3]Hugh Ross, "Astronomical Evidences for the God of the Bible," posted on the Reasons to Believe website, <www.reasons.org>. Abridged version of *The Fingerprint of God* (Orange, Calif.: Promise Publishers, 1989).

[4]Don DeYoung and Richard Bliss, "Impact 200: Thinking About the Brain," posted on Institute of Creation Research website (February 1990) <www.icr.org/pubs/imp/imp-200. htm>.

[5]Chuck Colson and Jack Eckerd, *Why America Doesn't Work* (Dallas, Tex.: Word, 1991), pp. 36-37.

[6]Job 9:4-11; 11:7-9; 37:3-7; Psalm 8:3-5; 19:1.

Chapter 14: Endurance
[1]At my request, Grace shared her story with me through a written account that she calls *Beyond Human Power.*
[2]Psalm 66:12; Isaiah 40:12-31.

Chapter 15: Perspective
[1]Monique shared her story with me in a personal interview in November 2001.
[2]Neil T. Anderson, *The Steps to Freedom in Christ* (Ventura, Calif.: Gospel Light, 1996), p. 4.
[3]Romans 12:19-21; Psalm 55:18; 140:7; Proverbs 21:31; 1 Samuel 17:47; 2 Chronicles 20:15; Psalm 143:12; Isaiah 25:8 KJV; 98:1; 1 Corinthians 15:57; 1 John 5:4.

Chapter 16: Tenacity
[1]Psalm 17:6; 27:7; 50:15 paraphrased; 55:16; 56:9; Romans 8:31 paraphrased; Psalm 61:2; 86:5; 91:15 paraphrased; 119:146; 120:1; 145:18.